Pioneer Airline Pilot

the life and times of

Capt. E.H. "Bill" Lawford, A.F.C.

by

Hayden K. Lawford

Published by: Hayden K. Lawford
                40 London Road
                Hurst Green
                Etchingham
                East Sussex TN19 7QP
                United Kingdom

       Tel: +44(0)1580 860257

       email: hayden.lawford@hursthome.fsnet.co.uk
              hkl1940@eircom.net

ISBN 0-9545118-1-6
EAN 9780954511814

Printed and bound by CPI Antony Rowe, Eastbourne

Further copies of this publication are available from the author at the above address

© Hayden K. Lawford 2006

By the same Author:

"In Galway Skies"   ISBN 0-9545118-0-8, published 2003

Pioneer Airline Pilot

Introduction	*iv*
The Pioneer Years	*1*
The Great War	*16*
Airco and Aircraft Transport and Travel Ltd	*35*
The First Week	*44*
Pioneer Airline Pilot	*64*
A Change of Course	*89*
The Golden Era at Croydon	*106*
Psychic Experiences and the R.101 Disaster	*119*
World War Two and Retirement	*130*

Appendix 1: The Aircraft Transport and Travel Traffic Book

Appendix 2: Logbooks

Appendix 3: Aircraft operated by Aircraft Transport and Travel

Appendix 4: Britain's First Airline Pilots

Appendix 5: Documents

Appendix 6: Air Ministry Traffic Officers and Wireless Operators

Appendix 7: Aircraft types flown by Bill Lawford

Hounslow Heath, 25th August 1919. Bill Lawford stands in front of the Airco 4a, G-EAJC before Departure for LeBourget A painting by Terence Cuneo, commissioned by British Airways plc, 1979
Reproduced by kind permission of British Airways plc

Foreword

Cruising above the weather in the relative comfort of a Boeing or an Airbus, today's air traveller would find it difficult to imagine the claustrophobic atmosphere of the enclosed passenger compartment of an "Air Express" en-route to or from the Continent back in 1919. That's if the traveller was lucky enough to enjoy the extra comfort of the enclosed cabin instead of enduring two or three hours of being battered by the aircraft's slipstream in an open cockpit wrapped up in heavy leather flying clothing. Such was the lot of the first airline passengers who were prepared to pay huge fares for the privilege. The first commercial passenger aircraft were noisy, unpressurised, unheated and draughty, you sat in a wicker chair with no seat belt, possibly clutching an optional packed lunch as there was no cabin service or flight attendant, possibly surrounded by small parcels containing urgent freight. Few aircraft had toilet facilities, but the pilot might deviate from the normal route on request to give you a bird's eye view of places of interest. In bad weather you might find yourself flying only 50 feet above the surface in order to remain clear of low cloud because the pilot needed to see the ground in order to navigate by reference to prominent landmarks, the development of instrument flying, radio navigation aids and radar was still a long way in the future. Using contemporary sources I hope that I have been able to describe what it was like to travel on the early airlines and recount some of the experiences of the first airline passengers and pilots, together with the story of Britain's first international airline company, Aircraft Transport & Travel Ltd.

This book is also a biography of my father, Capt. E.H. "Bill" Lawford AFC, who began his career in aviation at pioneer Hendon during 1910, and later became proprietor of a Flying School at Brooklands. Following service with the Royal Flying Corps and the Royal Air Force he joined Aircraft Transport & Travel Ltd. as a pilot, and later became a well known personality in the Control Tower at Croydon Airport during the 1920's and 1930's. I was fifteen years of age when he passed away in 1955, and so was too young to have learned much about his aviation career at first hand, but I do remember that he was proud to have been one of the select band of airmen that had served with the R.F.C. in France. It was my father's enthusiasm for all things aeronautical that inspired me to pursue a career as a pilot. I recall many of my father's old aviation friends visiting him during the last years of his life when he was invalided by a series of strokes. Later I discovered that many of our visitors were pioneers of civil aviation, but names such as Warren Merriam, Willie Armstong and O.P. Jones meant little to me at the time - if only I had been a few years older and possessed my present interest in aviation history at the time!

Twenty years on I began sorting and studying my father's Flying Logbooks and collection of photographs and papers in detail. My research continued intermittently over the years, but retirement has at last allowed me to complete this biography. I learned much during my researches about pioneer flying before the Great War, the work of the R.F.C. Corps pilots in France during 1916, and the everyday flying experiences of the early airline pilots.

My father was one of the first pilots to be employed by Aircraft Transport and Travel Ltd, (A.T.&T.), and an account of this company's efforts to establish a reliable airline service forms an integral part of this biography. Unfortunately nearly all A.T.&T.'s company records have been lost, and there is little information about the everyday operations of the airline, but I hope that I have succeeded in telling some of the story. The classification of flights operated by A.T.&T. following the lifting of restrictions on 25th August 1919 is unclear, and I hope that after perusing contemporary documents and reports that I have been able to piece together a factual account of the start of Britain's first regular civil international airline service. Handley Page Air Transport and the Instone Airline have only been mentioned in the context of the A.T.&T. story, an omission which is not intended to detract in any way from the important contribution made by these companies to the pioneer British airline industry.

I have also recounted my father's time at Croydon Airport, the pre-war Airport of London. A tremendous camaraderie existed amongst the small community of aviation professionals working in the in the fledgling civil aviation industry between the Wars. Many came together to form the Guild of Air Pilot's and Navigators, an organisation which continues to play an important part in advancing standards within the aviation industry today. The death of the first Master of the Guild, Sir W. Sefton Brancker, in the R 101 airship disaster, deeply affected my father and his colleagues. Some looked to spiritualism to ease their grief, and I have included my father's accounts of his experiences of aviation related psychic phenomena.

I hope that this book will give an insight into the life and times of one of Britain's early aviation professionals.

Hayden K. Lawford

The Pioneer Years

Eardley Hayden Lawford, later better known as "Bill", was one of four sons and three daughters born to Anne and John Eeles Lawford, the proprietor of the firm of Lawford and Sons Ltd, suppliers of brick, lime and cement, with branches in Camden Town, Paddington and Kilburn in north west London.

Back in 1739 Bill's great, great, great grandfather, John Lawford, a carpenter by trade, had become a copyhold tenant of the Manor of Bushey, Hertfordshire, and successive generations of the family succeeded as manorial tenants until after the death of Bill's great grandmother, Ann Eeles Lawford, in 1833 when the tenancy was relinquished and the assets divided equally between her nine children. Following the loss of the tenancy at Bushey her son, John Eeles Lawford, moved from Bushey to Camden which was then on the northern outskirts of the London conurbation. The Lawford's had always been a practical family, working as blacksmiths, carpenters and farming their holdings at Bushey, and John Lawford soon found employment as a slater working in the London suburbs.

By 1840 John had set up the business of Lawford and Sons Ltd. at New Road, Camden. The new business prospered, and by the time of Bill's birth on 21st September 1884 it was a sizeable concern supplying lime, sand and other building materials at a time when the London suburbs were rapidly expanding into the adjacent countryside. After attending Aldenham School, Hertfordshire, from 1897 to 1900 Bill joined the family business. He was nineteen years of age when, on 17th December 1903, the Wright Brothers made the first successful powered flight by an aeroplane. Six years later the Wright's headline making visit to Europe created enormous interest in the new science of aviation and Bill, who was already fascinated by early motor cars and petrol engines, eagerly read reports of the flying machines being constructed by aviation pioneers such as S.F. Cody, A.V. Roe and Geoffrey deHavilland. Like many young men at the time he had joined the Territorial Army becoming a member of the 1st Victoria and St.George V.R.C. London from 1901 to 1908, and qualifying as a mounted infantryman. S.F.Cody's experiments to explore the potential use of balloons, airships and kites for military purposes were of particular interest to Bill and he spent many hours reading about the mysteries of the internal combustion engine and studying mechanics and engineering. He was convinced that the early aeroplanes would soon become a practical flying machines, and as early as October 1907 he made a prophetic £1 wager with a colleagues, C.R. Towers, that:

"In October 1912 there will be an aeroplane, i.e. a balloonless flying machine, that will fly against a 40 mile per hour wind."

There was little official encouragement for the handful of dedicated British aviation pioneers and the construction of the first British aeroplanes was often driven by the hope of winning one of the major cash prizes on offer and the possibility of interesting the government in the military potential of the aeroplane. During 1910 Lord Northcliffe, owner of the "Daily Mail", offered a prize for the first aeroplane to fly from London to Manchester. A leading contender for this prize was the famous French pilot Louis Paulhan, who had set up his headquarters in a large shed situated on some large fields at the end of Colindale Avenue, Hendon. This site had already been used by Mr. E.J. Everett for flying experiments, and was just a couple of miles along the Edgware Road from the Lawford family home in Brondesbury Park, giving Bill the opportunity to watch Paulhan's preparations at first hand. The site had been leased by Paulhan's sponsor, Mr. George Holt-Thomas, a successful newspaper owner and industrialist, who had recently obtained the British agency for Maurice Farman aircraft and would later form the Aircraft Supply Company, better known as Airco. Holt-Thomas was to become a major player in the British aircraft industry and his companies would provide employment for Bill and many of his comrades in the fledgling airline industry following the Great War. At dawn on 27th April 1910, Louis Paulhan took off from Colindale in gusty weather to complete the first flight from London to Manchester and claim the £10,000 prize. The fields that Paulhan had used as his base were leased later that year by his rival and runner-up in the London to Manchester race, Claude Graham-White, and opened as Hendon Aerodrome on 1st October 1910.

Graham-White's business partner and manager of the new Hendon Aerodrome, Richard Gates, soon organised a series of weekend air races at the new venue, drawing huge crowds of spectators to watch the exciting new sport of flying. Hendon soon became a magnet for Bill, and he spent many hours watching the exploits of the early aviators and studying the latest flying machines.

During 1911 Bill took his first flight at Hendon in a Valkyrie Monoplane belonging to the Aeronautical Syndicate, the first company to take up residence in the famous row of Sheds which housed such famous aviation concerns as A. V. Roe, Bleriot and Graham-White Ltd. The Valkyrie Monoplane had an unusual configuration. A canard monoplane with a pusher propellor, it had been developed by the well known pilot and founder of the Aeronautical Syndicate, Mr Horatio Barber, and had been flown at Hendon as early as 1st

Valkyrie monoplanes at Horatio Barber's Aeronautical Syndicate, 1911

via Richard.T. Riding

October 1910. Three different versions were built, a single seater powered by a 35 hp Green engine, a two seater with 50 hp Gnome engine and a three seater with a 60 hp Green engine. By May 1911 a total of five Valkyries were flying at Hendon, and Horatio Barber had presented four of the machines to the Government for evaluation by the Military. The Aeronautical Syndicate had also opened a flying school at Hendon, and by July 1911 at least one Valkyrie had been fitted with an early form dual control, and this may have been the aircraft in which Bill took his first flight. Fired with enthusiasm following his Valkyrie flight Bill was determined to learn to fly for himself and gain the Royal Aero Club Aviator's Certificate, popularily known as the "Ticket". This was an expensive proposition at the time, but Bill had decided that a career in the family business of Lawford & Sons was not for him, leaving the business to pursue his goal of becoming an aviator.

Unfortunately the Aeronautical Syndicate ceased trading in April 1911 after giving flights to over 150 passengers during the previous twelve months, and Bill now had to look for an alternative flying school. A well known Scottish aviator, Mr. W.H. Ewen, who had obtained his "Ticket" in February 1911 and subsequently opened a successful flying school in his native town of Lanark in Scotland, had recently relocated his flying school to Hendon Aerodrome, where it opened for business during January 1912 operating Bleriot, Deperdussin and Nieuport monoplanes for training. The Ewen School was to become one of the busiest and most successful schools at Hendon, training both civil and military pilots, and Bill Lawford was one of the first pupils to join the new school. He commenced training during January 1912, and was soon able to perform "straights" in Ewen's 28hp Bleriot monoplane.

Opportunities for flying at Hendon during the early months of 1912 were severely curtailed by severe winter weather, but by early April "Flight" was able to report:

"Miss Prentice, and Messrs. "Edmund", Lawford and Gist were all handling the Bleriot confidently and showing marked progress."

Subject to weather, aircraft reliability and the availability of instructors, it was possible for aspiring pilots to complete the tests for the R.Ae.C . Certificate after only three weeks of training, but the majority of pupils took much longer to reach this level of proficiency. Dual control aircraft were rare, as it was generally considered that aspiring pilots would gain greater confidence by learning to handle the aircraft unaccompanied. Consequently great emphasis was placed on ground instruction, simple manoeuvres were explained, often with the help of aircraft like structures mounted on adjustable trestles to demonstrate the effect of controls and familiarise the pupils with the different flight attitudes. Taxiing and "Rolling" practice would then follow, with the pupil gradually increasing the aircraft's speed before attempting "Straights", short flights made across the aerodrome just a few feet above the ground.

Bill Lawford in a 28 hp Deperdussin of the W.H.Ewen School, Hendon

E.H.Lawford Archive

After becoming proficient at "Straights" the pupil attempted half-circuits, followed by left and right hand figures of eight, all flown within the boundaries of the aerodrome. The early aircraft used for training, such as the Bleriot and Deperdussin, were underpowered and very basic often without any flight instruments. Lateral control was achieved by means of "wing-warping" which presented a real challenge to the novice pilot as it produced a strong adverse yaw against the direction of roll. Opportunities for the tyro pilot to practice in these aircraft were limited to calm weather, and consequently most flying practice took place during the early morning or late evening when surface winds were light. The aviation periodicals "Flight" and "The Aeroplane" carried weekly reports on the activities at the new flying schools and the progress being made by individual pupils. On 12th April "Flight" reported:

" *A very big day's work indeed was put in on Friday 12th April, the pupils being out with the school machines almost continuously from 5am to 7pm. Ten of the pupils were on the ground all of whom got in some excellent work without any mishap beyond a broken wire. Miss Prentice is making excellent headway, rolling the full extent of the ground in absolutely straight lines, and Messrs .'Edmund', Gist, Ware and Lawford have thoroughly overcome the difficulty of keeping the machine in a true line.*

and on 13th April:

"In the evening the School machines were again out and Messrs. Lawford, 'Edmund', Baumann and Miss Prentice and Lieut. Kerrich got in some good rolling and flying." On Sunday morning M. Dubois and Baumann and Lieut. Kerrich were out at 5.30 am getting in some good practice. In the evening M. Baumann made a very nice flight on the Bleriot, and Lieuts. Kerrich and Pennycuik got in some excellent straights. "Messrs .'Edmund', Lawford and Miss Prentice were all handling the Bleriot confidently and showing marked progress."*

On 2nd May Ewen took delivery of a second Caudron aircraft powered by a more powerful 45hp Anzani engine. Up to this time he had personally supervised most of the flying and consequently training was often interrupted when he was away on business in connection with the Caudron agency. With an increasing demand for flying training Ewen employed Marcel Desoutter as his assistant instructor, allowing his pupils to take full advantage of the improving weather conditions and longer daylight hours. On 21st May it was reported that:

"After a trial flight by Marcel Desoutter, a new instructor of the School, Messrs. James, Apcar, Lawford, Ware, Edmund, Major Skipwith and Capt. Chamier put in a good amount of work rolling and flying starting at 4am, with breaks only for breakfast and lunch pupils out all day."

At the end of August Dubois left the Ewen School to join the French Military Flying Corps, and in early September he was replaced by Sydney Pickles as assistant instructor. Pickles was an Australian national and had gained his Aviators Certificate only six weeks earlier. His employment resulted greater availability of instruction at the School. The first R.Ae.C. Certificate to be awarded to a pupil from the Ewen School was granted on the 3rd September 1912 to a Swiss national, Edouard Baumann. Baumann would later become one of the best known flying instructors in England and later opened his own Flying School. Bill continued to make further progress with the Deperdussin monoplane during the autumn of 1912, and in October it was reported that:

"Mr Lawford is doing good straight flights at 20 feet and making nice landings"

He soon progressed to half-circuits, and on 15th November put in 2 hours practice, followed on the 21st by twelve straight flights in the 35 hp Caudron after Pickles had flight tested the machine.

The following day Mr. W.F. Lewis Turner joined the Ewen School as instructor and Chief Pilot. Turner was one of the most experienced instructors of the time and he soon produced further successes for the School. Seven pilots from the Ewen School had obtained an Aviators Certificates by the end of 1912,

The W.H. Ewen School, Hendon, April 1912:
T.S. Apcar, Miss Dorothy Prentice, E.H. "Bill" Lawford, Dubois, W.H. Ewen and Gist seated are Warren and Edouard Baumann, who would later become one of the best known instructors at Hendon

Courtesy of the Flight Collection

The Ewen School, 1912, showing from left to right the new Caudron Biplane, a Caudron Monoplane, and the School Bleriot and Deperdussin monoplanes

"Aeroplane"

and six of these had qualified during the autumn after Ewen had engaged Pickles and Turner. Sydney Pickles experience on the Caudron biplane was now gaining him a growing reputation as a display pilot, but this was to have unfortunate consequences a few months later.

During December 1912 Bill began flying the 35hp Caudron, continuing his training under Lewis Turner, soon progressing through half-circuits to circuits and figure "8's". On 8th March he flew several circuits, finishing on each occasion with a nicely judged landing, and on 15th March he flew the all tests required to qualify for his Aviators Certificate on the Caudron. It was reported that:

> "Mr Lawford flew Brevet Test at 250 feet landing beautifully on the mark"

Bill was granted Royal Aero Club Aviators Certificate No. 442 on 18th March 1913, an internationally recognised qualification issued through the Federation Aeronautique International. It would be a further six years before a national system of pilot licensing was introduced. He completed the following tests to qualify for the R.Ae.C. Aviator's Certificate, witnessed from the ground by a Royal Aero Club observer :

A. Two distance flights, consisting of at least 5 kilometres (3 miles 185 yards) each in a closed circuit, marked out by two posts situated not more than 500 metres (543 yards) apart, the aviator changing his direction after going round each post, so that the circuit shall consist of an uninterrupted series of five figures of eight, and

B. One altitude flight, consisting of a minimum height of 50 metres (164 feet), but this must not form part of one of the two flights prescribed above. The method of alighting for each of the three flights should be with the motor stopped at or before the moment of touching the ground, and the aeroplane must come to rest within a distance of fifty metres (164 feet) from a point indicated previously by the candidate.

E.H. Lawford with 35hp Caudron after gaining his
Royal Aero Club Aviators Certificate, 13th March 1913

E.H. Lawford Archive

Royal Aero Club Aviators Certificate 442 granted to E.H. Lawford
13th March 1913

Pioneer aviation was now an increasingly popular spectator sport, and on most weekends during the summers of 1913 and 1914 large crowds flocked to Hendon to see famous aviators including Pegoud, Hamel and Hucks performing daring aerial "stunts" and competing for the many prizes on offer for pylon races. Capt Louis Strange had also learned to fly at the Ewen School during 1913 and stated in his memoirs that "Bill Lawford was often to be found working in the shops at Hendon".

Seeking opportunities to use his newly gained qualification Bill visited the great centre of pioneer British aviation and motor racing at Brooklands, searching for a suitable business venture in aviation, where he met the pioneer French aviator Maurice Ducrocq, who had qualified for Aviators Certificate No. 23 on 21st October 1910. As a result of the growing demand for flying training Ducrocq had given up his job teaching French and opened a flying school at Brooklands early in 1911, using a 50 hp Gnome powered Henri Farman "Boxkite" aircraft with a front elevator, which he had purchased for £620 from the estate of the Hon.C.S. Rolls following his untimely death in a flying accident at Bournemouth. Ducrocq also held the British concession for the French Nieuport monoplane which was also used at the school. Initially, business at the Ducrocq School was slow, and it was not until 26th of October 1912 that Ducrocq's young mechanic, John Alcock, became the School's first pupil to qualify for an Aviators Certificate. John Alcock continued to fly at Brooklands as a sporting and test pilot up to the outbreak Great War, and seven years later, with Arthur Whitten-Brown as navigator, he would pilot the first aeroplane to complete a non-stop flight across the North Atlantic.

A Caudron Biplane belonging to the Ewen School at Hendon. This is may be the aircraft that Bill Lawford flew for the grant of his RAeC Certificate

via Richard T. Riding

In the spring of 1913 Bill became a partner in Maurice Ducrocq's Flying School, and a new company, Ducrocq and Lawford Ltd, was registered on 7th May 1913 with a nominal share capital of £3000 divided in to £1 shares and an address at 17, Ironmonger Lane, London E.C. The flying school was re-named the "Ducrocq & Lawford School", based in Shed No.14 at Brooklands. During the summer months Bill gained further experience flying as an instructor at the school, giving lessons in the school's ageing 50 hp Henri Farman to a number of pupils including T.K. Wong, Roger and V. Gaskell-Blackburn. The Ducrocq and Lawford School remained active until mid July 1913, when the Henri Farman was withdrawn for a major overhaul and a badly needed re-cover with new fabric.

Bill was keen to purchase a better aircraft for the school as the Henri Farman was now becoming obsolete and he had been impressed a new French pusher biplane, the "Champel", powered by a 100 hp Anzani engine, recently flown by Monsieur Champel at the Juvisy Aerodrome, near Paris. Champel had recently established four new World records for an aircraft carrying four

Maurice Ducrocq seated on his 50 hp Henri Farman biplane

Jean Ducrocq

Bill Lawford in the rear cockpit with Sydney Pickles standing in the front cockpit of the new two seat Champel biplane shortly after their arrival at Hendon

E.H. Lawford Archive

passengers with his latest machine at Cercottes in France. He arrived at Brooklands during August to promote his new two seat machine powered by a 100 hp Anzani engine, but shortly after his arrival the Champel was involved in a minor collision with a Parsons Aeroplane being taxiied by John Alcock. Fortunately, only minor damage was sustained by both aircraft and was soon repaired.

Impressed by the new Champel, Bill made arrangements to purchase the aircraft, for use by the Ducrocq and Lawford School, and to demonstrate the aircraft to potential customers. He engaged the services of Sidney Pickles, his former instructor at the Ewen School, who was now a well known display pilot, to fly the Champel from Brooklands to Hendon to demonstrate the aircraft on the evening of the 20th September 1913 following the finish of the second Aerial Derby. The Race was won by Gustav Hamel, and the weather was ideal for the many demonstration flights that were available after the event. Towards dusk Mrs.Cheridah de Beauvoir Stocks requested a flight in the Champel. Mrs Stocks had been the second woman to obtain an Aviator's Certificate in Britain, and at the time was the only active lady pilot in Britain.

Mrs. Cheridah DeBeauvoir Stocks

E.H. Lawford Archive

Sidney Pickles took off in the Champel with Mrs. Stocks as his passenger, flying low around the pylons marking the race course at about 300 feet, but as he applied left rudder to make his usual tight left-hand spiral turn before landing, the Champel's rudder bar jammed with full left rudder applied and the aircraft entered a steep bank and began to descend rapidly in a tight turn. Pickles desperately tried to reduce the bank angle and applied full power, pulling the stick fully back, but this had little effect, the rate of descent and rotation increased and the aircraft crashed into the ground behind the megaphone box from a height of about 60 feet. Pickles and Mrs.Stocks sustained serious injuries and subsequently spent many weeks in hospital. Pickles later stated that the rudder had jammed when the heel of his left shoe became wedged between the rudder bar and the cockpit floor, causing loss of control. The situation was aggravated still further as Pickles applied full throttle just before the Champel crashed. The steep gliding turns, referred to as "spirals", which Pickles often executed to loose height, provided ideal flight conditions for a spin, the mechanics of which were not fully understood at the time, and it is probable that the Champel entered a spin at low altitude from which recovery would have been impossible. Mrs Stocks never flew again. Sydney Pickles suffered a compound fracture of his right leg and a serious body wound and it was six months before he returned to the sky again.

The loss of business following the grounding of the Henri Farman and the crash of the Champel proved a severe financial blow for Bill, and resulted in the demise of the Ducrocq and Lawford Flying School. The Company's solicitor wrote to the Registrar of Companies on 25th November 1913, requesting that it be removed from the Register, as the Company had no assets or creditors and only one remaining shareholder, and early in 1914 the Company was wound up. Maurice Ducrocq later found employment as a Test Pilot with Vickers, under Percy Muller, who had obtained his Aviators Certificate at the Ducrocq School and had been appointed manager of the Vicker's works at Weybridge. The wreckage of the Champel Biplane was stored in the cellar of the Lawford family home at Brondesbury Park for many years, but the 100 hp Anzani engine was salvaged and used in Bill's next business venture, the two seat Wong Biplane.

Tsoe K. Wong, an Australian born Chinese, had joined the Ducrocq and Lawford School at Brooklands on 10th July 1913 to continue his flying training. Wong had arrived in England from China to study the latest developments in aviation and engineering, and by 1912 he was learning to fly with the B.H. England Flying School at Shoreham Aerodrome on the Sussex coast, where he began construction of a single seat biplane of his own design, named the *"Tong Mei"*, or "Dragon Fly", powered by a 40 hp ENV engine. After crashing at Shoreham while attempting to master the B.H. England Flying School's Collyer-England biplane, Wong moved on to Brooklands with his uncompleted *"Tong Mei"* aircraft where he met Bill Lawford and on the 10th July he resumed his flying training at the Ducrocq and Lawford School on the Henri Farman biplane. When this aircraft was grounded later in the month for repairs, Wong transferred to the Bristol School at Brooklands qualifying for his Aviators Certificate 593 on 15th August 1913.

Wong was seeking financial backing to develop a two seat version of the *"Tong Mei"* biplane, and on 20th November 1913 the company of T.K. Wong Ltd was registered, with a share capital of 2000 shares of £1 each and a registered address at Bill's accountants, Messrs. H. Graham King, of 17, Ironmonger Lane, London E.C, who also handled the affairs of Ducrocq and Lawford Ltd, to build and develop a two seat version of the *"Tong Mei"*. The directors of the new company were T.K. Wong and Bill Lawford, and on 25th November an agreement was signed whereby T.K. Wong sold the original *"Tong Mei"* to the Company for £750, receiving 750 shares in the Company in lieu of payment. Bill received 375 shares in the Company as payment for the 100 hp Anzani engine No. 1517, recently salvaged from the wreck of the Champel biplane. At the time the uncompleted single seat *"Tong Mei"* was in storage at 36 Willesden Lane, N.W, and assisted by Bill, Wong immediately began work on the conversion of this aircraft into the two-seat biplane. During his time at the Bristol School, Wong had met Robert R. Skene who had qualified for Aviator's Certificate 568 and was now an instructor at the School. Wong was seeking further investors for the *"Tong Mei"* project and Skene introduced him to his brother, William F. Skene, who agreed to become the third investor in T.K. Wong Ltd. during February 1914, purchasing 750 shares of £1 each in the Company.

E.H. Lawford, T.K. Wong and W.F. Skene with the Wong two seat Biplane, Brooklands, 1914

E.H. Lawford Archive

By early 1914 the conversion of the original "Tong Mei" to two seat configuration and the installation of the 100 hp Anzani engine had been completed and Wong carried out preliminary test flights at Brooklands. A novel feature of the new aircraft was the two small celluloid windows in the fuselage sides, just aft of the engine, and the unusual diagonal cross-bracing of the fuselage structure. Little is known of the history of the aircraft during it's time at Brooklands. Following the outbreak of the Great War in August 1914 all civil flying in Britain was placed under the direct control of the government, and both Bill and William Skene gave up their civilian activities to enlist in the Army. Wong left England and travelled to the Federated Malay States where he set up an aviation service company using Avro 504's. The Wong two seater was shipped to Malaya, where it crashed at Kuala Lumpur Racecourse, Selangor, during a demonstration flight in 1915. The company of T.K. Wong Ltd. was finally dissolved in 1919.

The golden age of pioneer aviation at Hendon and Brooklands ended abruptly with the outbreak of War on 4th August 1914. The early aviators did not usually keep records of their flying experience, however Bill estimated that by the outbreak of the Great War he had obtained about 150 hours flying experience on Henri Farman, Bleriot, Deperdussin, Caudron and Champel aircraft.

The Great War

By the autumn 1914 the misplaced optimism that it would "all be over by Christmas" had evaporated and the British Expeditionary Force was digging in along the Western Front. Inspired by the wave of patriotism that swept the country following Kitchener's call-to-arms, Bill wrote to the War Office on 13th October volunteering for the Royal Flying Corps:

"Sir,
    If there are any vacancies for Subalterns in the Royal Flying Corps, will you kindly forward full particulars of qualifications necessary for selection? I have had two and a half years of practical aviation - and ten years petrol motor experience. My "Brevet" is No. 442, gained on 18th March 1913 - Caudron Biplane. I have also had seven years Mounted Infantry Service, during which period I was always a "Marksman" shot. I am a British born subject. My age is 30 years on Sept. 21st 1914. I can produce undeniable credentials and have very many friends and acquaintances who are officers in the R.F.C. If it be impracticable to offer me a commission, I am willing and anxious to serve in any other capacity or with any other branch of the service working in conjunction with the R.F.C. - such as Royal Engineers - Army Service Corps - Motorcyclist Dispatch Carrier or the like, as I am very eager to get to the "theatre of war" as soon as possible. My motorcycle is at your disposal. May I ask for a reply at your earliest convenience."

    The War Office was quick to respond as men with experience of airframes and engines were urgently required for the fledgling R.F.C., and on 23rd October Bill transferred from the Territorial Army to the Royal Flying Corps, reporting to Farnborough as R.F.C. No.1877, Air Mechanic 2nd Class. At 30 years of age he was older than many of his comrades, and with the experience that he had gained in the Territorials he was soon posted to France, arriving at the R.F.C. Headquarters, St. Omer, France on 25th November 1914.
    The R.F.C. numbered just over 2,500 officers and men at the time and was engaged in reconnaissance and patrol work for the Army using a variety of hastily assembled aircraft types. This was a relatively quiet period on the Western Front, and the front line was now virtually static following the mobile battles of the late summer and autumn and the retreat from Mons. The First Battle of Ypres had ended in stalemate, and both sides were now settling in for the static trench warfare that would dominate the following four years of the conflict.
    Bill was posted to No.5 Sqdn which had been one of the first Squadrons to arrive in France following the outbreak of war, and was part of No. 2 Wing R.F.C. formed on 29th November 1914 to operate with the 2nd and 3rd Army Corps. Bill's new comrades were not inclined to greet him by his unusual first

name of "Eardley", so he soon became known as "Bill", a nickname which would stay with him for the rest of his life.

5 Squadron was based at St. Omer with detached flight at Ballieul and was engaged in carrying out reconnaissance flights for the 3rd Army Corps and also occasional bombing raids over the lines. The Squadron was equipped with Henri Farman aircraft, a type with which Bill was familiar from his time at Brooklands, and 80 hp Avros. The under powered Farmans were handicapped by their slow groundspeed when flying into a strong wind and were replaced by Martinsyde Scouts in mid December 1914. This period of inactivity on the front resulted in plenty of drilling and route marches carried out with the objective of maintaining the men's fitness. Despite poor weather the Squadron made the first photographic reconnaissance flights during December using a fixed box camera which provided very useful information for the artillery.

Traditional celebrations took place on Christmas Day 1914 and every officer and man was presented with a gilded metal box containing Christmas greetings and a small ration of cake and chocolate from H.R.H. Princess Mary. This was literally the calm before the storm as on the night of the 28th December a violent wind damaged 30 aircraft on the ground at St. Omer and Ballieul, nearly half the R.F.C.'s total aircraft strength in France. The stormy weather continued over the New Year, and Bill and his comrades were kept busy servicing the Squadron's aircraft the open air in all weather conditions. This unsatisfactory situation improved on the 11th January when the Lille Road aerodrome at Ballieul became waterlogged and the detached flight moved to the nearby "Cemetery" aerodrome where the aircraft were housed in temporary sheds. The Squadron was now involved in early artillery observation experiments, using aircraft equipped with W/T equipment, but on 23rd January Bill, who had been promoted to Corporal, was posted back to England where a letter from the Assistant Director of Military Aeronautics at the War Office awaited him:

"Sir,
A few first class pilots are required at the Aeronautical Inspection Department for test flying, and if you are prepared to consider such employment you should place yourself in communication with the Chief Inspector, Aeronautical Inspection Department, South Farnborough, from whom full particulars can be obtained."

The Aeronautical Department of the War Office were probably unaware that Bill was already serving in the R.F.C, and as a result of his enthusiasm to enlist the previous autumn he had missed this opportunity. For now, even though he held the pre-requisite RAeC Aviator's Certificate required for all intending R.F.C. pilots, Bill would have to wait before being called for R.F.C. pilot training as only officers and N.C.O.'s were being accepted at this time. The R.F.C. would grow by more than 13,000 men during 1915, and many officers were transferring from other regiments to the R.F.C. for pilot training. The under funded training facilities were hard pressed to cope with the increasing demand for pilots, and even with a civilian "Ticket" Bill was more valuable to the RFC as a ground instructor, spending the next 7 months serving in this capacity at Netheravon and Farnborough.

Following his time as a Technical Instructor Bill was promoted to Sergeant and posted to No.1 Reserve Aeroplane Squadron, Jersey Brow, Farnborough. His Commanding Officer was Major F.F ."Ferdy" Waldron, who had been one of the first R.F.C. pilots to fly to France at the outbreak of hostilities, and was later killed in action commanding 60 Squadron in 1916. Bill already had about 150 hours flying experience before joining the R.F.C, and he began military flying on the Caudron G.3 Biplane, a similar machine to the Caudron which he had flown at Hendon before the war. He had completed four hours flying on the Caudron by the end of August 1915, which he recorded a service issue Pilot's Log Book, the first official record of his flying time.

Another aircraft type familiar to him was the Bleriot Monoplane, and he flew Bleriot 5604 on 9th September, commenting that his first landing was *"good but fast."* He corrected this a couple of days later with a *"much slower landing"*, but later in the day he made a forced landing after running short of fuel in misty conditions and had to land the Bleriot in Long Valley near the Fleet Road, luckily with no damage to the aircraft. The following day he flew the Bleriot back to Farnborough.

Bill put his knowledge of aircraft rigging and engines to good use during his flights in the Bleriots and Caudrons, noting any unusual handling characteristics in his log book. But unfortunately his flying for 1915 came to an abrupt end on 10th October when the engine of Caudron G.3, 5264, failed after take-off from Farnborough. Bill log recorded:

"Engine stopped at low altitude over Officers Mess - was obliged to turn <u>downwind</u> in order to land in Aerodrome. Machine sideslipped in gust, turned over on landing, and was wrecked."

Turning back following an engine failure after take off to attempt a landing on the aerodrome is not recommended, and this Caudron was a well worn training aircraft which had seen better days. Bill was lucky to escape the crash with minor injuries, but it was two months before he was fit enough to return to duty in December. After resuming his duties he received promotion to Flight Sergeant, and was posted as a Technical Instructor to the newly opened No.1 School of Military Aeronautics at Reading. The Reading School was equipped with two old Martynside Scouts and an unserviceable 50 hp Gnome engine used as aids for ground instruction in engines and rigging, and once again

Bill put his technical experience to good use. Among his pupils were the future Air Marshals Robert Saundby and Trafford Leigh-Mallory[1].

On 9th February 1916 he returned to flying duties with No.1 Reserve Aeroplane Squadron at Farnborough, spending the next two months training in BE2c's fitted with dual control. In early April he was posted to 41 Squadron at Gosport for a week of ground training before more flying on Maurice Farman Longhorn and Shorthorn aircraft. A further posting to 45 Squadron at Thetford flying the BE2c followed. In mid May 45 Squadron moved to Sedgeford where operational training on the BE2c continued. After passing a night flying test, Bill qualified as one of the small number of N.C.O. pilots serving in the Royal Flying Corps when he was graded as First Class Flyer No.43 at the Central Flying School, Upavon. With a total of over 26 hours flown on service aircraft in addition to his pre-war flying Bill was a relatively experienced pilot at a time when newly trained R.F.C. pilots were often sent on active service to France with a total of less than 20 hours flying experience.

Following leave Bill was posted back to the B.E.F in France to serve with 7 Squadron, attached to the 2nd Brigade, operating BE2c's from Bailleul. The BE2c, known as "Stability Jane", was being produced in very large numbers and had become the workhorse of the R.F.C. It's stable flying qualities made it an ideal platform for artillery observation and aerial photography work, and when flown solo without an observer in the bombing role it could carry a load of one 110 lb bomb and four 20 lb bombs carried on under wing racks. However, it's poor manoeuvrability made it an easy target for enemy artillery and hostile aircraft. After a few days making familiarisation flights and practice bombing sorties Bill began his operational flying carrying out reconnaissance and Artillery Observation flights in the Ypres area. Artillery Observation flights by the Corps Squadrons provided vital information for the artillery batteries on the ground for the accurate targeting of enemy positions. The BE2 crews engaged in this work were frequently subjected to small arms fire at low level, and heavy anti-aircraft fire, known as "Archie." It was dangerous work which received little publicity unlike the exploits of the more glamorous "Scout" squadrons.

The R.F.C. at Bailleul occupied three adjoining landing grounds known as the Town, Asylum and East Aerodromes, with No.7 Squadron based at the Town Aerodrome. Shortly after taking off from this Aerodrome on the afternoon of 21st June with Lt. Stephens as observer in BE2c 2755 the engine lost power and Bill was forced to make an emergency landing at 1 Squadron's base on the Asylum Aerodrome. The cause of the problem was found to be a cracked cylinder which was quickly replaced and the aircraft was flown back to the Town Aerodrome that evening. Two days later on a regular patrol between St.Eloi and Picanton at 9000 feet he became lost in a thunderstorm for over 20

---

[1] See Appendix 5, page 1

minutes, encountering severe turbulence, but landed safely having seem plenty of gun flashes and anti-aircraft fire which he referred to as *"plusiers archies!"* This was the week before the Somme offensive, and as part of the preparations for the forthcoming attack the R.F.C. carried out frequent raids and reconnaissance patrols on enemy gun positions despite very unsettled weather.

On the early morning of 28th June, returning from a 2 hour reconnaissance patrol in BE2c 2623 over St.Eloi and Picanton with his observer Flt. Sgt. Weare, Bill became lost in the low cloud and rain, and the following afternoon he flew a patrol with a misfiring engine in continuing gusty winds and poor visibility.

Early on the morning of 1st July the continuous bombardment by the British Artillery of the German positions on the Somme ceased abruptly and the infantry went "over the top" into the lethal hail of German machine gun fire. Bill and Flt.Sgt. Weare took off on a reconnaissance of the northern sector of the front at 6.50am - the main action on the Somme was to the south of their normal patrol area around the Ypres salient, but on patrol at 10,000 feet they observed *"general activity and many archies"*. Two days later Bill made a special flight to Vert Galant with dispatches, taking-off at dawn and returning to Bailleul in the afternoon.

On 10th July BE2c, 2623, developed engine trouble which delayed a planned patrol for an hour. This particular BE2c was approaching the end of it's useful life and at the end of the month it was returned to the No.1 Aircraft Park at St. Omer, where it was found to be beyond economical repair and scrapped. Bill eventually got airborne at 7.30 am in a replacement BE2c with Sgt. Kilby as observer and noted considerable activity both in the air and on the ground. They spotted a hostile aircraft, probably an LVG, at 8,500 feet and gave chase but it fled over the lines being too fast for the BE2c to get within firing range.

At the time magnetic compasses were often unreliable and a few days later an erratic compass led Bill astray and he became lost behind the lines during an evening patrol in BE2c 5750. Fortunately, the weather was good and he was able to set course westwards towards the setting sun, crossing over the lines with a badly vibrating engine that was rapidly loosing power.

During a reconnassance patrol at 8000 feet on the evening of the 19th July he saw *"a mine sprung and tremendous artillery activity south of Armentieres"*. This was Bill's last flight with 7 Squadron and next day he was one of six additional pilots and aircraft posted to 5 Squadron, based at Droglandt, following a decision to increase the strength of this Squadron from 12 to 18 aircraft.

On the evening of the of 20th July Bill flew BE2c 2587 to the No. 5 Squadron aerodrome at Droglandt, between Cassel and Poperinghe, where major repairs were carried out to the aircraft including fitting a new tailplane, elevators, ailerons centre-section, left-hand upper wing and fuselage streamlining. The aircraft was test flown on 24th, but during the take-off some loose hay on the aerodrome caught on a wing tip which impaired the aircraft's handling, forcing Bill to land immediately before making two successful test flights during which a newly fitted radio installation was tested. This aircraft was a presentation aircraft, "Baroda No.8", and Bill would fly many missions in it during the next five months.

The summer weather of 1916 continued to be very unsettled, but the Squadron flew frequent patrols over the lines whenever weather conditions allowed. On 27th July Bill had to abort a flight after taking off in foggy conditions, recording that *" we were lost in mist at 200' but found aerodrome and landed O.K."* Another unplanned return followed on 31st when they ran out of fuel at 8000' over Ypres due to a leaking fuel tank but succeeded in gliding back to the aerodrome to make a deadstick landing.

The French and Belgian railway networks formed a vital part of the German military supply system and were an important target for the R.F.C. From the outbreak of the War 5 Squadron had carried out raids on important railway installations, and during August and early September 1916 it was engaged solely on attacking these targets. On 1st August Bill took part in a raid carried out by 16 BE2c's on the railway line loop at Ledenghem. Under heavy anti-aircraft fire he successfully dropped two 112lb bombs on the target causing extensive damage to the station, sidings and nearby ammunition dumps. During a raid on Zonnebeck on the 6th August Bill's BE2c was damaged by enemy fire. A spent enemy bullet was found in the fuselage following this raid which he kept as a souvenir. On 8th August he was one of eight BE2c's from 5 Squadron that attacked the railway sidings at Roulers during which he dropped a 112lb bomb on the target inflicting extensive damage on the rolling stock and sidings. This was followed by a raid on the 12th when a group of 9 B.E.'s attacked and badly damaged the sheds at Houthem used as enemy billets with 20lb bombs. He was flying BE2d 5755 on a raid during the evening of the 19th August when the engine suddenly failed:

"Engine, cylinder and piston seized up - smashed engine - dense clouds - unable to see between 7000' down to 1200' - forced landing at Eecke in cornfield, damaged leading edge."

Two days later he was forced to abort a flight soon after take-off because of a rough engine in BE2d 6254. On inspection it was found that the cylinders and a small end bush had loosened and there was a crack in the inlet manifold. Forced landings were a regular occurrence and were often due to poor maintenance and inspection procedures in the field. The Corps pilots risked their lives daily, flying war weary aircraft in hostile skies full of anti-aircraft fire and hostile aircraft. Following a photography sortie over the Ypres Salient Bill noted that the *"left-hand rear plane strut shot through by hostile aircraft unseen"*. Next day, on an artillery observation flight over the area, he encountered two hostile aircraft but succeeded in escaping their attentions.

The damage to the wing of BE2d 5755 following the forced landing on 19th was repaired by the 25th August, and after carrying out test flights Bill made further bombing raids with this aircraft. On 2nd September he encountered more bad weather - *"heavy rain clouds at 6000' or under. N out at La Gorgue, unable to see for one hour in clouds, all machines returned."* On the morning of 7th the Squadron attacked the enemy aerodromes at Beveren and Rumbeke near Roulers - *"Bombing, six 20lb bombs and two incendiaries on Roulers North and South Aerodromes. Machine hit with shrapnel also hostile aircraft."*

Engine problems continued into September. The poor condition of some of the engines fitted to the Squadrons BE2c's manifested itself again on 11th when the engine of BE2c 2587 failed yet again and Bill noted almost routinely - *"engine conked out and landed in aerodrome."* While testing this aircraft after repairs he narrowly avoided a crash - *"engine test - engine cutting out had narrow squeak over tree tops, just gained aerodrome - heavy landing to avoid another machine."*

The engine fitted 2587 continued to give trouble and Bill had another lucky escape on the evening of the 13th testing 2587 - *"engine test, cutting out very dangerous, just cleared O/C's hut into aerodrome."* The following morning after an abortive attempt to bomb Becaleare in 40mph winds and low clouds 2587 was tested yet again - *"Engine test. O.K. except cutting out at very low revs."*

Next morning he took-off in this aircraft with A/M Jones on a photographic mission behind the lines of the Ypres Salient but only 15 minutes into the flight the engine cut out again and Bill was forced to land in field near the aerodrome. Clearly there was a problem with this engine, but despite this Bill took-off on another raid in 2587 - *"Bombing - engine again cut out. Just gained aerodrome with 2 x 110lb bombs."* He was lucky as landing an aircraft carrying live bombs is a risky venture. After this incident a new engine was finally fitted to 2587 and it was successfully test-flown the following morning, but there had been some close calls.

On the evening of the 19th September 2587 performed well on a raid on Langemarck Railway Station with other aircraft of the 2nd Brigade, dropping two 112lb bombs, causing considerable damage to the station and railway lines.

Pilots generally preferred to fly the same aircraft whenever possible, familiarising themselves with an aircraft so that they would immediately notice any unusual behavior. Bill usually flew BE2c 2587 on his tour of duty with 5 Squadron, completing over 40 flights in this aircraft.

An Artillery Observation flight on 22nd September in 2587 with Sgt. Power as observer had a successful outcome - *"Looking for hostile 15" gun on train. Spotted bombed and machine gunned train at Poelcappel planing down to 4000' at V2a. A.A. very vigorous."* Next evening on a photographic sortie over the lines of the Ypres Salient with Lt. Duncan as observer the camera jammed, but they were able to drop two 20lb bombs on an enemy gun emplacement sited in a wood to the north of Boesinghe. On 24th Bill took part in a successful raid dropping two 110lb bombs on the ammunition dumps and railway sidings between Vyfwegen, Langemarck and Poelcappel, and two days later raided the railway sidings at Poelcappel again under heavy anti-aircraft fire.

After 10 days home leave Bill returned to France. During his absence 5 Squadron had moved from Droglandt to a new base at Marieux Aerodrome near Doullens, only 10 minutes flying time from the Somme front line, to replace 15 Squadron on artillery co-operation work with the Thirteenth Corps.

The Squadron operated in support of ground forces engaged in the final weeks of the offensive on the Ancre sector, but the autumn weather was already beginning to restrict operations. Bill's first flight from Marieux was a Flash

Bill Lawford, left, with a comrade and BE2c, 1916

E.H. Lawford Archive

Reconnaissance patrol with Lt. Edwards. Taking off at dusk they became lost for about 30 minutes, in the darkness returning from the patrol, but Bill eventually spotted the green lights of the Aerodrome and landed safely.

Early on 15th October Bill flew a successful Artillery Co-operation flight in 2587 for the 2nd Army and his observer, Lt. Goudie, drove off three hostile aircraft with the Lewis Gun. Patrolling the front with Lt. Duncan as observer on the 18th they spotted a new enemy gun battery, *"which our guns then severely strafed causing two fires in Puiseaux-au-Mont."*

The engine problems which had plagued 2587 at Droglandt now returned. On a three hour morning artillery observation flight with Lt. Duncan they were harassed by many enemy aircraft, and later Bill took-off again on an evening patrol, but was forced to return to base after 15 minutes with a cracked cylinder. Between operational sorties Bill carried out regular checks of the rigging and tail incidence of 5772 and test flew the aircraft. But the engine gave trouble on the 22nd when he was forced to return from a photographic sortie with Sgt. Shepherd 20 minutes into the flight - *"engine failure, 1425 revs & vibrating badly - returned"*. Undeterred, they climbed aboard 2587 and took-off again to continue their mission to photograph behind Puisieux and Miraumont, where large fires were observed, and dropped two 20lb bombs on Star Wood. The engine on 5772 continued to give trouble during a raid on Puisieux a few days later and they had to make another unscheduled return to Marieux - *"engine cut out, valve burnt out, forced landing just gained aerodrome - turned up wind at 50 feet. Very near shave!"*

November 1916 began with a spell of very poor weather and continuing problems with 5772. Bill's Flight Commander, Capt. Farrow, returned to England, and was replaced by Lieut. Trafford Leigh-Mallory, a former pupils of Bill's at the Reading School, later to become A.O.C. Fighter Command during the Second World War. Bill had applied for a Commission and Leigh-Mallory assured him that his application was being processed. On a patrol with Lt. Power near Beaumont Hamel during the afternoon of the 2nd November the engine of 5772 lost power yet again - *"unable to keep machine up in air, engine dud, revs 1300, staggered to aerodrome dropping all the time to under 300 feet."* They were airborne again fifteen minutes later in a replacement machine to continue observation of the barrage at Beaumont Hamel carrying out a successful patrol in spite of another rough running engine - *"continued successfully although the engine developed valve trouble - 2 valves burnt out. Crossed over "No Man's Land" at 1600 feet - many archies."*

The repairs made to the engine of 5772 were unsatisfactory as after two more test flights Bill made another forced landing the following day near the aerodrome. Two days of bad weather ensued and the time was used to fit and test a new quick release bomb mechanism to 2587, but this aircraft suffered a catastrophic engine failure next morning during an artillery observation flight with Sgt. Shepherd. Bill recorded:

"Forced landing near Bertrancourt, cylinder blew off, smashed piston and crankcase."

A repair crew was quickly summoned and installed and a replacement engine in record time. Bill flew the aircraft back to base that afternoon, but the problems continued after further checks and adjustments were made to the new engine over the next few days and it failed again on morning of the 14th November:

"Forced landing, 4 cylinders cracked - slept out with machine all night in field near Bertrancourt - one continual bombardment."

The aircraft was repaired in the field next morning and Bill flew back to Marieux later that day.

Puiseux was bombed again on an artillery observation sortie during which many enemy aircraft were seen and Bill experienced at first hand one of the many dangers faced by the Corps pilots and observers operating in a sky full of projectiles when he recorded:

"I distinctly saw and felt a shell pass the machine and followed it with my eye to enemy lines where it burst - Marvellous - but a true statement."

The stalemate on the Somme had continued during the autumn months and with the onset of winter the battle slowly ground to a halt. Flying activity was now severely curtailed by the weather, but the vital Artillery Observation flights continued whenever conditions allowed. Bill worked with 32 H.A.G. in early December, and made yet another forced landing in BE2d 5772 during a trench shoot with Lt. Power:

"Forced landing - 2 cylinders, 2 valves gone landed at Verrennes near Achieux. Stopped out with machine all night, 32 H.A.G. very helpful and hospitable to us - especially S/M Brown - Enemy shelling Achieux all night, unpleasantly near, some of the shells burst near us."

The aircraft had to be dismantled and returned to base by road. Little flying activity took place until 20th December, and Bill used this time to study for exams in morse code and photography. On the 20th he carried out a trench shoot with Lt.Power in 2587, severely damaging enemy trench 20K before dropping two 20 lb bombs on Rossignol Wood on the way home. He was forced to to abort a raid on Vaulx with two 110lb bombs on Boxing Day morning when 5772 developed engine trouble again:

"engine dud, had to return and found magneto lead off also 3 other leads loose, the plug terminals having vibrated off."

An artillery observation and counter battery flight in BE2e 7158 over Puiseux that afternoon was successful, and they bombed Rossignol Wood again. Returning from Rossignol Wood the following day with Lt. Allen, Bill ran into enemy aircraft:

"I saw 7 or 8 hostile machines - chased one hostile machine nearly up to Achieux - dived under it and opened machine gun fire on it - at which machine fled back to "Hunland" being very fast - I think it was an "Albatross" - our anti-aircraft gunfire being terrific all this while - Hun machine was

evidently endeavouring to "Straff" our observation sausage balloons on which she apparently opened fire."

The Germans were now becoming more adventurous and the air superiority enjoyed by the R.F.C. during the second half of 1916 was about to end. Enemy aircraft now operated more frequently on the Allied side of the lines and the German Jasta units were re-equipping with the new Albatross and Fokker Triplane which would inflict heavy losses on the R.F.C. during the Spring of 1917. On 1st January 5 Squadron went into rest and Bill returned to Farnborough and was given leave. He had flown over 200 hours on operations during his time in France.

Reporting back from leave at the end of January 1917 Bill was posted as a test pilot to the Southern Aircraft Repair Depot at Farnborough. Aircraft returned from the Western Front for repairs were overhauled at this facility, and each aircraft was test flown to check performance and handling before being returned to service. During the next two years Bill would test many of the main aircraft types in service with the R.F.C. His experience on BE2's during his time in France now proved useful carrying out general handling and performance checks on many BE2's. Bill's logs show that the type usually took between 35 to 45 minutes to reach an altitude of over 8000 feet.

The R.F.C. in France was now suffering serious losses following the appearance of new German aircraft types such as the Albatross during a month which would be remembered as "Bloody April". However flying at Farnborough was not without it's own dangers including frequent engine failures caused by faults ranging from loose carburettor jets to ignition and bearing failure which together with the vagaries of the weather called on all the experience and skill of the pilots attached to the Test Flight.

Bill also tested the uprated version of the BE2c, the BE12, an unsuccessful attempt to turn the very stable BE2c into a manoeuvrable fighter aircraft. He also carried out climb and performance tests on the Armstrong Whitworth FK7, which took 40 minutes to climb to 13,000 feet, and on the Martinsyde which could make 10,000 feet in just over 22 minutes, considerably better climb performance than the lumbering BE2's. With the exception of climb performance checks these air tests cannot have been very comprehensive as they often lasted only 15 or 20 minutes for newly repaired aircraft.

In June 1917 the Archbishop of Canterbury visited Farnborough and an impromptue flying display was laid on for his benefit. Unfortunately, a heavy hail shower passed over the aerodrome while Bill was displaying an Armstrong Whitworth FK7, and he later described this flight as *"very painful!"*

At last, on 21st July, after many months of waiting, Bill was Commissioned to the rank of Second Lieutenant, and appointed to the Training Division, but his services were still required at Farnborough and he received further orders to remain at S.A.R.D. The routine life at Farnborough was occasionally interrupted with air raid warnings and occasional practice defensive patrols were flown by S.A.R.D pilots, but no enemy aircraft were encountered.

The test pilots were often called upon to deliver aircraft to Lympne Aerodrome in Kent for collection by Squadron pilots based in France, and during the autumn of 1917 many were also delivered from the depot at Farnborough direct to the No.1 Air Park at St.Omer by SARD test pilots to satisfy the increasing demand for replacement aircraft in France.

R.F.C. Test Pilots, S.A.R.D. Farnborough, 1917, Bill Lawford and Lt. Kirton on the right

E.H. Lawford Archive

During December 1917 Bill carried out a series of performance test flights on the DH 4 light bomber. Some of these tests were carried out at high altitude without oxygen equipment, and it could take up to an hour and a half to reach an altitude of 18,000 feet. On 13th December, flying DH4, C4518, from Farnborough, with Cpl. Hughes as observer, Bill climbed to 20,350 in an hour and 20 minutes, the final 350 feet taking 8 minutes, giving a final rate of climb of about 40 feet/minute. Bill and his observer must now have been experiencing the effects of hypoxia - oxygen starvation. Although it was well known at the time that pilots could lose consciousness in the rarefied air at high altitude, the insidious effects of hypoxia which causes loss of judgement and euphoria were not fully understood. This was probably the reason for their rapid descent out of control from 20,000 feet. Bill had been flying above a thick cloud layer and it was an hour and a half since he had taken off from Farnborough. There was a strong northerly wind at altitude which had carried them off-course and they had no idea of their position. Bill described the incident:

> *"We were lost in clouds for over an hour - finally came down to 80 feet in order to see anything - when I discovered I was over the sea - turned north for fifteen minutes when I at last saw land at 80 feet, which proved to be the Isle of Wight, impossible to see above that height owing to dense clouds and sea mists. Effected a perfect landing but struck a rut just as machine was stopping, which turned machine over damaging top-planes, rudder, propeller, and fore part of fuselage. Engine missing badly and threatening to cut-out all the time during the descent from 20,000 feet - extraordinary luck that we did not fall into the sea."*

It had been a lucky escape. The engine problems encountered during their descent through cloud were probably caused by ice forming in the induction system of the engine as it cooled during the rapid descent through the humid air towards the sea. Without modern gyroscopic flight instruments to guide him Bill had been lucky to keep the DH 4 from entering a spin and he was lucky to regain visual contact with the surface over the sea and not to have impacted the mist enshrouded high ground of the Isle of Wight with fatal consequences. The next three days were spent salvaging the damaged aircraft, and he arrived back in Famborough four days later.

Bill tested many different aircraft types over Christmas 1917, including the SE5A, which he found a delight to handle. The winter weather continued to cause problems. Ferrying a DH 4 to Penshurst Bill became lost in a snowstorm. Emerging from the blizzard he found himself miles off course over the south coast near Worthing and as it was dusk he decided to land in a field. He took off for Penshurst the following day with orders to collect an SE5A for delivery to Lympne, but the weather deteriorated after he landed at Penshurst and he was grounded for another day before flying on to Lympne, taking four days to make a journey normally completed in less than a day.

The routine work of testing and delivering badly needed aircraft to the Squadrons in France continued during the spring of 1918. On the 1st April the new Royal Air Force was formed by the amalgamation of the R.F.C. and R.N.A.S, and Bill received further promotion to the rank of Flight Lieutenant in the new Service. On 18th April 1918, in spite of atrocious weather and gale force winds, Bill and three colleagues volunteered to deliver four urgently needed SE5A's from Farnborough to Marquise near Calais. These were the only aircraft to cross the Channel to France that day, and next day a letter was received at Farnborough from the Director of Parks and Depots at the Air Ministry:

> *"In connection with the flight made by the undermentioned officers, yesterday, when they volunteered to take a certain number of machines over to France that were most urgently required by the Expeditionary Force, I am very*

glad to note that four were safely delivered, and consider this a particularly noteworthy effort.

Lieut. Carroll,   Lieut. Lawford,   Lieut. Kirton,   Lieut. Linley,   Lieut. Scott

I would request that you be good enough to convey to the Officers concerned, and in particular to Lieut. Carroll, my sincere thanks for this work, and congratulations upon this splendid effort.

It will probably interest them to know that the Expeditionary Force were most urgently requiring machines of this type, and were highly satisfied at getting some delivered yesterday."

F.C. Jenkins, Brig.General

Bill checks out a BE 12 at Farnborough

E.H. Lawford Archive

Testing the SE 5a was extremely popular amongst the S.A.R.D. pilots and the aircraft's handling was highly rated by all, providing plenty of opportunities to perform aerobatics in a front line aircraft. In contrast to the SE5a was the large twin engine Handley Page 0/400 bomber which Bill had his first experience of handling during May. After spending some time at the controls he commented that *"they are very heavy but easy"*. By the autumn he had also flown the Bristol Fighter and made a forced landing at Stonehenge en-route from Farnborough to Bristol - *"carburettor very loose - studs pulling through causing air leaks and distributor adrift also terminals off on magneto - machine conked-out."* Engineers were sent from Farnborough to repair the "Brisfit", but arrived with the wrong inlet manifold, so Bill returned to Farnborough to ensure that the correct parts were dispatched to the crippled aircraft. A few days later a broken rocker arm resulted in another forced landing in an Armstrong Whitworth FK 7 after take-off from the airfield at Oxford, but the aircraft was soon repaired and Bill flew on to Farnborough without further incident. Climb checks made with a Sopwith Dolphin recorded a climb to 5000' in 4 minutes 10 seconds and an indicated airspeed of 115mph at 5000' and 9 minutes 40 second to reach 10,000' with an indicated airspeed of 106 mph.

Lt. Lawford and Lt. Carroll give their opinion about the condition of the aircraft to be ferried to France

E.H.Lawford Archive

The cessation of hostilities on 11th November 1918 following the signing of the Armistice was widely celebrated, and many "Joy Rides" were given to the ground personnel at S.A.R.D, followed on the 16th by a Service of Thanksgiving at Farnborough. But the celebrations were marred a few days later when Bill's colleague, the popular Lieut. Peg Kirton, crashed in a Sopwith Dolphin and later succumbed to his injuries.

By the end of November 1919 Bill had tested a total of 922 aircraft at S.A.R.D, comprising 59 different types and variants, and he now had a total of 910 hours flying experience. Flying at Farnborough continued at a more relaxed pace following the signing of the Armistice. On New Year's Day 1919 Bill was awarded the Air Force Cross in the New Year's Honours, and on 27th January he was posted to the 86th Wing, No.1 Communications Squadron at Hendon Aerodrome where he had begun his flying career seven years earlier. This posting would decide the future direction of his flying career. No.1 Communications Squadron was formed in December 1918 after the Air Minister, Lord Weir, had experienced four forced landings in France while

Bill Lawford in SE5a, Farnborough 1918

E.H.Lawford Archive

being flown from London to Paris in an R.A.F. aircraft. As a result, the Foreign Office requested the Air Ministry to form a dedicated R.A.F. Squadron to provide reliable transport between the two capitals for personnel and documents in connection with the peace negotiations taking place at the Palace of Versailles, near Paris. This Squadron later became known as the cradle of British air transport, and many of it's pilots would later find employment with the pioneer civil airlines. The Commanding Officer of the Squadron, Major Cyril Patteson, had already surveyed the London - Paris air route for the Air Ministry, and the Squadron's pilots included Alan Campbell-Orde, later Operations Manager of B.O.A.C., Jerry Shaw, Charles McMullin and many more who would later play a major part in the development of the British airline industry. Flights between the two capitals began during December 1918, initially using DH 4's, and later the larger twin-engine Handley Page 0/400's which could carry 10 passengers.

Bill made his first flight for the Communications Squadron on 13th February flying DH4, B7969, from Hendon to Buc Aerodrome, Paris, carrying official mails for the Peace Conference. During the 2 hours 55 minute flight the Rolls Royce Eagle engine gave trouble - *"engine spluttering over the Channel and onwards - magnetos dirty, L.H. Pump "Dud", gravity "Dud" - very little petrol left, arrived OK"*

The engine problems were fixed the following day, but bad weather kept Bill on the ground at Buc for two days and he had the opportunity to enjoy a night-out in Paris with a visit to the Folies Bergeres. On 17th he took-off at 3.10pm in B7969 loaded with mails from the Peace Conference to return to Hendon, but he encountered bad weather over the Channel - *"weather very bad approaching the French coast - driven down by clouds to 500' over the Channel - could not see English coast, clouds down to 50' at Penshurst, flew back to Lympne, but aerodrome above clouds and mist. Tried to land three times at Lympne - finally landed all O.K. at Hythe, School of Army Gunnery & took mails by train to London where I duly delivered same O.K. at 7pm. Altogether a very sticky trip indeed, could see nothing for rain clouds."*

Airco 4a F5764 of the Communications Squadron

"Airco" Photograph

This account of an early flight between London and Paris gives an insight into the difficulties faced at the time by the first pilots to make regular flights between the two capitals, however valuable experience was being gained in the operation of a regular air service, and this would be put to good use later in the year when the first international civil air services began. Wintery conditions continued until the end of February, and it was not until the 24th that Bill was able return to Hythe with Alan Campbell-Orde in a DH 4 to retrieve B7969 and return the aircraft to Hendon. Bill had another opportunity to fly the large twin-engine Handley Page 0/400 in early March when he took over the controls of D8326, H.M. Airliner "Silver Star", under the command of Capt. Chadwick.

H.M. Airliner "Silver Star"

A Court of Enquiry had been convened following death of a Communications Squadron pilot, Capt. Hacklett, who had perished when he crashed after leaving Hendon for Buc in a DH 4 on 26th February with one passenger, Lt.Graham of the Ministry of Shipping. Bad weather had forced Capt. Hacklett to divert to Hounslow and he had crashed while attempting to land at the aerodrome. Fortunately his passenger survived, and Bill was one the team appointed to inspect the crash site and investigate the circumstances of the accident. He also attended Capt. Hacklett's funeral at Heston before his next flight from Hendon to Andover with Lieut. Foden in the Handley Page 0/400, D8335. An uninvited passenger was discovered aboard the flight and the mysterious stowaway was put off the aircraft during an en-route stop at Andover. From Andover they flew on to Lake Down near Salisbury where Bill made his first landing on the type. This was followed on the 18th by his first trip from Hendon to Buc in the 0/400 "Silver Star", carrying Labour Members of Parliament to the Peace Conference with the C/O of No. 2 Communications Squadron, Major McCrindle, who would later become the Managing Director of the pre-war British Airways Ltd, and Capt. Chadwick, Chief Pilot of the

Squadron. Bill spent next two weeks based at Buc Aerodrome, Paris with this Squadron, making local test and sightseeing flights, to show V.I.P.'s including Fiesal, King of Hejas[2], the famous Paris landmarks .

The DH 4 aircraft initially used by the Communication Squadrons were open cockpit biplanes and passengers were carried in the gunners position behind the pilot. This was not at all popular as the passengers had to don heavy leather fur-lined flying coats, helmets and goggles as a protection against the cold of an open cockpit. This prompted George Holt-Thomas's company, Airco, to modify a number of DH 4's by adding a small enclosed cabin to the rear fuselage which could accommodate two passengers in reasonable comfort. To compensate for the aft movement of the C.of G. the aircraft's upper wing was re-rigged to eliminate the forward stagger of the standard DH 4. During his stay at Buc Bill flew as a passenger with Lt."Jim" McMullin in one of the newly converted DH4a's, H5894, piloted by Lt. George Powell. These pilots would join Aircraft Transport and Travel Ltd. later in the year. On completion of his temporary posting to Buc, Bill returned to Hendon in early April in a DH 4 flown by Alan Campbell-Orde with official mails, and on 16th April he was posted to No.1 Communications Squadron. During April this squadron had moved it's London base from Hendon Aerodrome to Kenley in Surrey, a more suitable location for the London base as aircraft would no longer be forced to fly over the built-up areas of the London suburbs en-route to and from France.

The routine work of flying the Handley Page 0/400's "Great Britain" and "Silver Star", now officially known as "H.M. Airliners", and other Communications Squadron aircraft between Kenley and Buc, continued through the spring of 1919. On 9th May Bill flew Handley Page 0/400, F3750, from Buc to Kenley carrying important documents. This mail contained the first German replies to the Allied Peace Proposals and among the passengers on the flight was Dr. Nansen, the famous polar explorer. The following day Bill recorded his one thousandth flying hour, a considerable amount of flying experience for the time. He made his last flight for the R.A.F. piloting H.M. Airliner "Great Britain" from Buc to Kenley. The flight was not without incident as the fabric covering stripped off one of the aircraft's propellors after take-off and Bill had to return to Buc where a new propellor was fitted before the flight continued on to Kenley in fine weather without further problems.

Bill was demobilised on 17th June 1919, as part of the massive run-down of the armed forces following the cessation of hostilities, and joined the many ex-service pilots hoping to continue flying in civil aviation.

---

[2] Now Saudi Arabia

Airco and Aircraft Transport and Travel Ltd

During the spring of 1919 the legislative and infrastructural framework necessary before civil aviation could begin again was put in place. There had been minimal government regulation of aviation prior to the outbreak of the War in 1914. National sovereignty over Britain's airspace had been established by the Air Navigation Act of 1910, which declared the air above His Majesty's dominion to be inviolate. The military had showed little interest in the use of aircraft prior to 1914 and aviation had developed as an experimental and sporting pastime, stimulated by the large cash prizes offered by newspaper proprietors and other commercial interests. In 1909 the Royal Aero Club introduced an informal qualification, the Royal Aero Club Aviators Certificate, which was granted to pilots who successfully completed a series of simple tests under the rules of the Federation Aeronautique International, the international body founded in 1905 to regulate sporting aviation.

The Great War had resulted in the rapid development of the aeroplane as a fighting machine, and large aircraft manufacturing concerns such as George Holt-Thomas' Airco and Handley Page Aircraft Ltd. had produced thousands of aircraft for the armed forces under Government contracts. With the ending of hostilities huge numbers of military aircraft became surplus to requirements and many of these became available for disposal on the civilian market. Around 20,000 ex-service pilots were demobilised over an eighteen month period, but at most only 1000 would find employment in civil aviation. Foreseeing the chaos that would result if ex-service personnel and aircraft were allowed to operate in an unregulated environment, the Government extended the ban on civil flying until 1st March 1919 in order to allow time for new legislation to regulate civil aviation to be enacted.

Back in October 1916 George Holt-Thomas had registered an aircraft operating company, Aircraft Transport and Travel Ltd., as a subsidiary of the Aircraft Manufacturing Company, Airco. Prior to the outbreak of the War Holt-Thomas had campaigned for the establishment of a powerful British Air Arm, and had engaged the talented young aviation pioneer Geoffrey deHavilland as Chief Designer at Airco. During the War Airco had expanded to become the largest manufacturer and supplier to the Government of aircraft and their associated components, and Holt-Thomas, foreseeing that the demand for military aircraft would collapse when hostilities ceased, sought to develop interest in his products for the civil market. He advocated the post-war development of air transport and was instrumental in persuading the Prime Minister, David Lloyd-George, to set up the Civil Aerial Transport Committee in May 1917,

"to study the development and regulation of post-war aviation for civil and commercial purposes from a domestic, imperial and international standpoint."

Chaired by Lord Northcliffe, The Civil Aerial Transport Committee was drawn from a wide spectrum of military, aviation, transport and industrial experts including Major W. Sefton Brancker, Capt. J.C. Porte, Brig. Maitland, H.G. Wells, Frank Pick MP, and Lord Trenchard.

In February 1918 the Civil Aerial Transport Committee published recommendations that there should be Government assistance for air transport, Empire air routes should be established, and an International Aeronautical Convention should be convened to decide the future freedom or otherwise of the skies over the sovereign states that would be used by international air transport. Meanwhile, the Air Ministry should take responsibility for the regulation of domestic air transport and the licensing of pilots and engineers. Following on this report a cautious Government agreed to provide a basic infrastructure of aerodromes, hangar space, emergency landing grounds, meteorological services and a free wireless communications system, all of which already existed under military control. However it ignored the Committee's recommendation that the first civil airlines should receive subsidy, an omission which would have serious repercussions for the fledgling British air transport industry.

Holt-Thomas addressed the Royal Aeronautical Society on the future potential of air transport during May 1918, and in November, following the signing of the Armistice, he appointed Brigadier Festing as Managing Director of his new air transport company, Aircraft Transport & Travel Ltd, and announced that the company would be ready to start a regular air service for passengers and freight between London and Paris as soon as government restrictions on civil flights were lifted. Frederick Handley Page also announced his intention to operate a regular air service between London and Paris. On the Continent, domestic flights had already commenced in Switzerland, France and Belgium and civil flying had been sanctioned in Gemany. During January 1919 Winston Churchill, recently appointed as the first Secretary of State for Air, announced that draft legislation to regulate civil aviation was being formulated, and that a Department of Civil Aviation had been set up within the Air Ministry under a Controller-General, Major General Frederick Sykes, who would have direct access to the secretary of State for Air.

Holt-Thomas now appointed Major Sefton W. Branker as a Director and General Manager of Aircraft Transport and Travel Ltd, and also a Director of the parent company, Airco. Brancker had learned to fly during 1913, and during an exceptional military career he had served as Comptroller General of Equipment in the R.F.C. and later as Chief of Personnel in the R.A.F. He gave up a successful military career to join Holt-Thomas, believing it essential that Britain should be at the forefront of post-war civil air transport. He would later be appointed Director of Civil Aviation at the Air Ministry, and would play a major part in placing the British airline industry on a sound footing before his untimely death in the R101 disaster eleven years later.

On the 2nd February 1919 Aircraft Transport and Travel Ltd. began operating a freight service on behalf of the Belgian Government carrying parcel post from Hawkinge, near Folkestone, to Ghent. Because of the continuing ban on civil aviation this service was operated using Aircraft Transport and Travel owned DH 9 aircraft carrying R.A.F. markings and flown by Service pilots. This quasi-military operation presented an ideal opportunity for the A.T.&T. management to gain valuable experience in the practical operation of a regular cross-channel freight service. A second air mail service started on 3rd March when 120 Squadron R.A.F. began flights between Hawkinge and Maisoncelle in support of the British Army of Occupation in Europe.

On 23rd February the new Air Navigation Order received Royal assent, paving the way for civil aviation to recommence, but there was some uncertainty following a surprise announcement on 1st March that the ban on civil flying in Britain would continue in force for a further two months. In the ensuing confusion an illegal charter flight was made from Hendon to Brussels by an unidentified aircraft allegedly carrying the Managing Director of Harrods.

The ban was temporarily lifted for the Easter Holiday celebrations when the Air Ministry permitted limited local joyrides to be operated at selected aerodromes. Both Aircraft Transport & Travel at Hendon and Handley Page at Cricklewood took advantage of this opportunity, but the general prohibition of civil flying continued until 1st May.

On the eve of the removal of the ban, the Air Ministry published the new Air Navigation Directions in the in the "London Gazette", detailing the procedures for the Registration of Aircraft, Airworthiness Certification, Overhaul and Examination, Pilot and Navigator Licensing, Rules of the Air, Signals, Prohibited Areas, import, export and control of aircraft. The first examinations for the issue of the new "B" Pilot Licences which would now be required for commercial flying were held that day, the candidates having to become familiar with the new directives in record time in order to sit the exams within a few hours of their publication. The basic framework permitting civil flying "within the Realm" was now in place allowing operations to commence next day.

Unsurprisingly, the national newspapers were first to take advantage of the lifting of the ban on the 1st May 1919. In the first few minutes of the new day an Airco 9, G-EAAA, flown by H.J. Saint of Aircraft Transport and Travel Ltd. took-off from Hendon bound for Bournemouth with one passenger and an early edition of the "Daily Mail". Unfortunately Saint crashed in poor weather at Portsdown Hill, Hampshire, luckily with no fatalities. Handley-Page had secured a contract to fly newspapers from London to Manchester and Edinburgh, and later in the day a Handley Page 0/400, flown by Lt.Col. Sholto-Douglas, left Cricklewood Aerodrome carrying 11 passengers bound for Edinburgh via Manchester. Manchester was reached in 3 hours after an uneventful flight, and Sholto-Douglas took-off the next day for Edinburgh but was forced to return due to bad weather, eventually reaching Edinburgh on 5th May. British commercial aviation had got off to an uncertain start.

The new industry escaped a potentially serious setback when an Airco 4A of No.2 Communications Squadron carrying the Controller-General of Civil Aviation, Major General Sykes, crashed at Kenley Aerodrome on 3rd May with an overheated engine. The pilot, Capt. E.M. Knott, lost his life but fortunately Sykes survived with minor injuries. Bill was still serving with the Squadron and he witnessed the incident which was later found to have been caused by loss of coolant due to an improperly secured radiator cap.

Before his discharge from the R.A.F. Bill sat the technical examinations for the issue of the new civil Pilot's "B" Licence, and was granted Licence No.150 on 12th June 1919, endorsed for B.E. Types, F.E.2B & 2D, Avro 504K & 536, Airco 4, 4a, 9, 9a, & 16, Armstrong Whitworth F.K.3 & F.K.8, Bristol Fighter and Handley Page 0/400, permitting him to pilot these types for hire and reward. His recent experience of air transport operations with the R.A.F. Communications Squadrons, together with over 1000 hours flying experience in more than 40 different aircraft types stood to his credit at a time when few ex-service pilots had more than 250 hours experience. On 16th June he was successful in gaining employment as a pilot with Airco's subsidiary company, Aircraft Transport and Travel Ltd. (A.T.&T.). Under Brancker's guidance A.T.&T. was actively recruiting pilots already familiar with the London - Paris route from the R.A.F. Communications Squadrons. One of these pilots was Lieut. Henry "Jerry" Shaw, who had been demobbed in early June, was appointed as Chief Pilot of Airco and it's associate company, A.T.& T. Shaw commenced flying for Airco on 8th June, giving joy rides at Harrogate in the DH 9b, K109, before flying this aircraft to Hendon a couple of days later. At Hendon Shaw began a series of test flights in the DH10, E5557, and also the Airco 16 prototype, K130, which he flew for the first time on 17th June, making test and demonstration flights with this aircraft over the next ten days. Bill had flown with Jerry Shaw during his time with the Communications Squadrons and would have known many of the new pilots now joining Airco from the Squadrons.

June 1919 was a relatively quiet period for A.T.&T. at Hendon. The company was beginning preparations for the start of international services to the Continent, but two months would elapse before the lifting of the ban on regular international flights. Domestic air services operated by A.T.&T's competitors had met with limited success, and with the exception of the Folkstone - Ghent parcels service operated on behalf of the R.A.F. the Company's revenue flying consisted of ad-hoc charter and pleasure flights ahead of the start of regular international services in late August.

In the tradition of the pre-war sporting aviation meetings the first post-war Aerial Derby was held at Hendon on 21st June 1919. Airco entered a highly modified DH 4, designated DH 4R, powered by a 450 hp Napier Lion engine, which had only flown for the first time that morning. Nevertheless this aircraft won the race piloted by Capt. Gerald Gathergood, completing two circuits around London at an average speed of almost 130 mph. Gathergood also piloted the Company's first business charter four days later when he flew Mr. Gordon Selfridge, Managing Director of the famous London store, to Dublin in the Airco 9b, K109.

An early photograph of the Airco 16 prototype, K130, later G-EACT, before application of registration marks

"Airco" photograph

On 28th June there were widespread celebrations following the German acceptance of the terms of the Peace Treaty drafted at Versailles. Bill celebrated the occasion by making his first flight as a pilot for A.T.&T. when he took two Airco mechanics on a 35 minute pleasure flight around Hendon Aerodrome in the new 4 passenger Airco 16 prototype, K130. Aircraft Transport & Travel was now assembling a fleet of aircraft supplied by it's parent company Airco for use on the forthcoming air services to the Continent. At the end of June 1919, the fleet comprised the Airco 9b, K109, the new Airco 16 prototype, K130 and additionally the two racing DH 9R's which had generated valuable publicity for Airco products following their success in the Hendon Aerial Derby.

Preparations for the launch the London-Paris air service intensified during July 1919 and Bill busied himself assisting with this work at both Hendon and Hounslow. The Air Ministry had ruled out A.T.&T.'s main base at Hendon aerodrome to the north of London as a terminal for continental services as it was considered unsafe to operate regular passenger services across the built-up areas of the capital, which would force aircraft to make a long detour around the London suburbs. In accordance with it's policy of selecting future civil aerodromes for international air transport from existing military sites the Air Ministry had announced that the R.A.F. Aerodrome at Hounslow Heath would be designated as the "London Terminal Aerodrome", and soon A.T.&T. staff from Hendon began to move in to the recently vacated R.A.F hangars and buildings at the new base.

The Air Ministry had also announced that as part of the celebrations following the signing of the Peace Treaty, civil flights would be permitted between the London Air Terminal at Hounslow and Le Bourget Aerodrome, Paris, from 13th July for one week only. The "Daily Mail" reported:

"Thanks to the efforts made by the British air authorities in Paris an agreement has been arrived at between the British and French governments permitting civil aerial intercourse between Britain and France from today until next Sunday. This is for the benefit of those who wish to see the Allied Victory Parade. The only restrictions are that the appointed landing places are Hounslow and LeBourget on the outskirts of Paris. The coasts must be crossed between Folkestone and Dungeness on one side and between Calais and Boulogne on the other. Civilian passengers must carry Passports. No goods are to be carried and aeroplanes are not allowed to fly over either London or Paris."

A.T.&T. took full advantage of this opportunity when Col. Pilkington, Managing Director of the well known glass manufacturing company, approached the Company's hire department with an urgent request to fly him to Paris in time for an important business appointment the following day as he had missed the boat train to Paris. A.T.&T. quickly arranged for Jerry Shaw to fly Pilkington to Paris in the Airco 9b, K109, and at 7.30 am on 15th July Shaw took off from Hendon with his passenger for Le Bourget Aerodrome, Paris. The new requirement to land at Hounslow for Customs and Immigration clearance seemed of little consequence to Shaw, who had often made the flight to Le Bourget as an R.A.F. pilot and was undeterred by the fact that he did not possess a Passport. As he flew over Cricklewood Aerodrome he spotted an aircraft from a rival company, Handley Page Air Transport, preparing to depart. Fearing that he would be delayed or even prevented from completing the flight without the necessary documents and that the Handley Page aircraft would be first to arrive at Le Bourget to claim the honour of being the first commercial civil aircraft to complete a flight between the two capitals, Shaw ignored the requirement to land at Hounslow for Immigration and Customs clearance and continued on through low cloud and rain direct to Le Bourget, where he landed at 10.15 am, spending over 20 minutes en-route searching for a break in the low clouds to clear the Beauvais Ridge. Landing on the military side of the Aerodrome he hoped to avoid the inevitable bureaucratic problems that would arise following his arrival without documentation. He had many friends amongst the French Air Force personnel and they were able to satisfy the queries from the civilian authorities on the far side of the Aerodrome about his arrival, which allowed Shaw and his passenger to complete their journey into Paris by tram and metro with the minimum of delay. This was the first officially sanctioned international passenger charter flight to be operated by a British company using a civilian aircraft and pilot. Shaw flew back to Hendon with Major Pilkington next day, but this time he landed at Hounslow for Customs and Immigration clearance, where he had explain why he had failed to report there on the outbound flight.

Later in the month, as part of Airco's sales drive, Jerry Shaw and Bill demonstrated the Airco 16 prototype to Swiss aviation representatives at Hendon. A.T.&T also operated a series of flights to the Goodwood Race Meeting and Bill spent a few days based at Tangmere, near Goodwood, arranging landing facilities. The A.T.&T. fleet continued to increase, and Airco products were on display at the First International Air Traffic Exhibition, E.L.T.A., held at Amsterdam in early August 1919. Bill left from Hendon on 6th August flying the A.T.&T. Airco 9b, G-EAGY, with an Airco mechanic, Mr. Canter. After clearing customs at Hounslow they flew on to Amsterdam with a refuelling stop at Marquise, near Calais, arriving at a very waterlogged E.L.T.A. Aerodrome after a flying time of 3 hours 30 minutes from Hounslow. Bill spent the next 12 days at Amsterdam demonstrating Airco aircraft at the E.L.T.A exhibition, where the fuselage of the second Airco 16, later registered G-EALM, was displayed on the large Airco stand in the main exhibition hall, together with a scale model of Hendon Aerodrome, a Napier "Lion" engine and a model of the Hucks Starter. During the show Bill flew the Airco 4A, G-EAHG, from the E.L.T.A. Aerodrome to Soesterberg for evaluation the Dutch military, returning to Amsterdam with Airco 9b, G-EAGY.

Airco 9b G-EAGY, demonstrated at the E.L.T.A.. Exhibition held at Amsterdam, August 1919
The A.J. Jackson Collection at Brooklands Museum

On 18th August he returned home as a passenger aboard the "Big B.A.T." K167, piloted by Major Chris Draper, who nearly 40 years later would achieve notoriety by flying an Auster aircraft under six of London's bridges over the Thames. Also on board the "Big Bat" was the aircraft's designer, Frederick Koolhoven, who Bill had known at Hendon before the War. After refuelling at Marquise they flew on towards Hendon, but were forced to divert to the R.A.F. aerodrome at Waddon because of poor weather conditions en-route.

Following the publication of the International Convention on Civil Aviation on the 21st July the Air Ministry announced that agreement had been reached with the French authorities, and that regular commercial flying would be permitted between London and Paris from 25th August onwards, and following his return from the E.L.T.A. Exhibition, Bill was involved in the final preparations for the start of the new service to Paris. As part of these preparations Jerry Shaw, who had remained at Hendon during the E.L.T.A. Exhibition to carry out test and photographic flights for Airco, flew from Hendon to Hounslow on the 12th August in the Airco 9b, G-EAGX, carrying A.T.&T's Chief Engineer, H.M. Woodhams, and stores for the new A.T.& T base. On the 16th he made a test flight in the newly refurbished ex-military Airco 4A, G-EAJC, during which the windmill driven starboard petrol pump seized. Shaw commented that the aircraft was nose heavy, but on 19th August, after a further test flight the aircraft was granted a Certificate of Airworthiness. Later that day Shaw delivered 'JC to A.T.&T at Hounslow, returning to Hendon in the Airco 4R, K142. Following a final test flight by Shaw on 21st August Airco 4A, G-EAJD was granted a C of A, and next day he delivered this aircraft to Hounslow.

The A.T&T fleet now comprised eight aircraft. Certificates of Airworthiness had been obtained for the four ex-Service Airco 4A's, G-EAHF, G-EAHG, G-EAJC and G-EAJD which were now ready for service together with the prototype Airco 16, K 130, and the three open cockpit Airco 9b's, G-EAAC, G-EAGY and G-EAGX. Pilots included Chief Pilot, Lieut. Jerry Shaw, Major Cyril Patteson, Lieut. "Jim" McMullin, Capt. Gerald Gathergood, Capt. Alan Riley, Capt. O.R. Baylis, and Lieut. Bill Lawford, the only one of these pilots to have flown in the pioneering era before the Great War. All had served with the R.A.F. and continued to use their service rank, although seniority also appears to have been determined by the date of joining the company. As Chief Pilot of A.T.& T's. parent company, Airco, Jerry Shaw's duties also included carrying out test and demonstration flights. Major Cyril Patteson, previously C/O of the R.A.F. No.1 Communications Squadron, had surveyed the London to Paris route for the Air Ministry in 1918. At nearly 35 years of age Bill was older than his colleagues and was one of the most experienced pilots in the company having gained extensive experience on a large range of service aircraft and engines during his time as a test pilot at Farnborough. Capt. Gerald Gathergood also had above average flying experience and had flown the Airco 4R to victory the 1919 Aerial Derby. Managing Director, Major General Sir Sefton Branker, and his deputy, General Manager Brigadier General Francis Festing, had held administrative positions in the military during the Great War. Consequently the company seems to have been run along service lines with a certain amount of military protocol and management practices evolved by the military which included the pilot's use of their service rank, and also drew on the valuable experience gained during the operation of the Folkestone - Ghent parcels service.

On Saturday 23rd August, the final preparations for the start of the regular service began when Lt. Jim McMullin left Hounslow flying the Airco 9b, G-EAGX, carrying spare parts for A.T.&T's Paris terminal at Le Bourget. The following day 120 Squadron R.A.F. operated the last flights of the regular air mail service between Hawkinge and Maisoncelle in Belgium. The way was now clear for the opening of regular commercial services between Britain and the Continent, and during the early morning of Monday 25th August staff at Hounslow and Le Bourget busied themselves with final preparations for the start of the new service, readying the Airco 4A, G-EAJC, Airco 16, K130, and Airco 9b, G-EAGX, for the inaugural flights of the new service.

Aircraft Transport and Travel Airco 9b, G-EAGX

Hillyer Collection, via Albert E. Smith and Croydon Airport Society

The First Week

On 23rd July 1919 the Air Ministry announced that the requisite number of countries had agreed to implement the terms of the International Convention for Aerial Navigation which had been drawn up as part of the Peace Conference at Versailles stating that:

"Pending the final signature of the International Convention, a provisional agreement to allow flying between France and Great Britain from Monday, August 25th has been arrived at between the respective Governments."

George Holt-Thomas was determined that Aircraft Transport and Travel Ltd. would be the first company to operate a regular air service to the Continent as soon as government restrictions were lifted. His company's exact plans for the first day of the regular service are unclear as A.T.&T.'s records came in to the possession of the Birmingham Small Arms Co. (B.S.A.) following that company's acquisition of Airco in 1920, and were later destroyed in an air raid during the Second World War. On 19th August 1919, the "Times" reported:

"The first regular international daily air service in the world will begin on Monday next between London and Paris, and vice versa, will start on this side from Hounslow. The service will run to LeBourget and at first it is the intention of the promoters of the venture to cater not so much for passengers as for light articles, with a view to proving ultimately that mails can be conveyed satisfactorily by the same means. The service is being run at midday so that business people in London, on reaching their offices at 9.30 or 10 o'clock in the morning, will have time to dispatch light articles to Paris where they will arrive before the offices and shops are closed."

One document of importance, the Company's Traffic Book[3], has survived, but this does not give the purpose of the three flights operated by the company on the first day of the London - Paris service. Not in doubt however is that A.T.&T was the first airline company in the world to operate a regular, scheduled, daily and sustained international civil air service carrying passengers and freight. Most of the passengers carried on the first day of the new service were newspapermen, some of whom were invited guests of the Company. George Holt-Thomas, proprietor of the Daily Graphic group of newspapers, had sought maximum publicity for his company's new service, but was not present at Hounslow to witness the departure of the first flights the regular service to Le

---

[3]See Appendix 1

Bourget. Norway, Sweden, Denmark, Switzerland and Holland had prohibited commercial flights across their territory by aircraft of the former enemy countries, and as they had not yet signed up to the I.C.A.N. Agreement Holt-Thomas called an international meeting of European airline representatives at the Hague, including representatives from Germany, to resolve this problem which threatened to delay the development of air transport within Europe. En-route to the Hague, he visited LeBourget to be present for the arrival and departure of the inaugural flights of the new service. A.T.&T.'s Managing Director, Sir Sefton Brancker, chaired the meeting of European airline representatives at the Hague which concluded on 28th August with the formation of the International Air Transport Association (I.A.T.A):

"to facilitate the commercial operation of long distance airways, especially in the north of Europe."

Surprisingly, the Chief Pilot of Airco and A.T.&T, Jerry Shaw, did not pilot any of the three flights operated on the first day of the new service. There are no entries for 25th August 1919 in his flying logbook[4], which shows that he made his first flight on the regular service the following day. As Air Ministry statistics for the service only begin from 26th August onwards, it is possible that the 25th August was regarded as a "Press Day" by the A.T.&T. management, with the object of gaining valuable publicity for the new service, and that revenue earning flights from Hounslow did not start until 26th August. Whatever the facts of this matter A.T.&T. chose three of their most experienced pilots to operate the first day's services. This was fortunate as the weather conditions on the route were quite unsettled, with areas of poor visibility, rain and a fresh south easterly-wind. The Company's Traffic book shows that the pilot of the 12.30pm departure, Major Cyril Patteson, did not fly on the route again for two months following his return from LeBourget to Hounslow on 26th August, whereas both Bill Lawford and Jim McMullin continued to fly regularily on the route. Patteson had been appointed as "Flying Manager" of the parent company Airco, a post similar to that of Operations Manager, and would have been busy organising the day to day flying activities for both Airco and A.T.&T. during this period. Airco's Chief Pilot, Jerry Shaw, was also busy making regular test, delivery and other special flights for Airco, but he also flew regularily on the London-Paris route. The two Companies were financially entwined as the salaries of the A.T.&T. pilots were paid by the parent company, Airco.

By the middle of the first week's operations the pilots were struggling to maintain the service in in the face of very severe weather conditions, but

---

[4]See Appendix 2

nevertheless only one flight was cancelled. This was a significant achievement, as one of the biggest obstacles that the new air transport companies had to address was to convince a sceptical business community that a reliable air service could be operated between the two capitals. Sir Sefton Brancker, Managing Director of A.T.&.T, paid tribute to the handful of pilots who had flown during the first week of the service when he commented some years later:

"they were probably better than any the world had seen before."

By the end of the week advance bookings for the London - Paris service looked promising, and a company spokesman declared that more passengers could have been carried had more aircraft been available. The one-way fare of 21 guineas (£22.05) or 42 guineas return (£44.10) included road transportation between the city centre and the airport, but it was only affordable by the very wealthy as it was more than eight times the equivalent first class rail fare from London to Paris at a time when the average weekly wage was between £3 and £5 for a tradesman and £10 for a professionally qualified person. Nevertheless, a total of 32 passengers were carried on the 14 flights completed during the first week.

Based on a study of the known facts and surviving documents there follows a detailed account of the flights operated on the first day of the service, and the first week's operation by Britain's first international airline company of the Worlds first international, civil, regular, sustained and scheduled air service for passengers and freight

Monday 25th August 1919

09:10 Departure from Hounslow to LeBourget

To ensure that the company would claim the honour of completing the first flight from Hounslow to Le Bourget following the lifting of restrictions on 25th August 1919, A.T.&T. arranged an early flight to LeBourget ahead of the planned timetable, setting a 9am departure time. As one of the company's most experienced pilots, Bill Lawford had already been involved in planning the service and he was selected to make this flight in the Airco 4A, G-EAJC. He carried a single passenger, a newspaper reporter, George Stevenson-Reece, representing the Evening Standard and the Daily Sketch, plus mixed freight including a consignment of leather, newspapers, several brace of grouse for the British Ambassador in Paris, Lord Derby, newspapers and pots of Devonshire Cream destined for the gourmet restaurants of Paris. Clearly A.T.&T were keen to show the advantages of air freight by including a consignment of perishable goods on the flight. These items were delivered from London by Carter Patterson and loaded aboard G-EAJC. Also aboard were greetings from the British Under Secretary of State for Air to his French counterpart, and urgent business documents.

Airco 4A, G-EAJC

The A.J. Jackson Collection at Brooklands Museum

The arrival at Hounslow just before 9 am of a Handley-Page 0/7 airliner G-EAAE, piloted by Major Leslie Foote, must have added some urgency to A.T.&T's preparations. Intense rivalry existed between A.T.&T. and Handley Page Transport for the honour of completing the first flight of day between the two capitals, and although it would be another week before Handley Page was ready to begin a regular service the company was intent on promoting future services and stealing A.T.&T.'s thunder by making the first flight of the day to Paris.

Major Foote departed from Handley-Page's Cricklewood base at 8.20am that morning, piloting G-EAAE on the short flight to Hounslow to obtain Customs clearance for a proving flight to LeBourget, carrying eleven journalists. However G-EAAE did not depart from Hounslow until 9.20am, and arrived at Le Bourget after 1.00 pm, well behind A.T.&T's inaugural flight operated by G-EAJC. To further publicise his planned services Handley-Page had also dispatched a twin-engine Handley Page 0/7 aircraft to Amsterdam earlier that morning under the command of Capt. Shakespear, who arrived at his destination in time for breakfast, before continuing on to Brussels for lunch, returning to Cricklewood in time for tea.

The A.T.&T. Airco 4A, G-EAJC, was ready for departure shortly after 9.00 am, and clearance was granted by Hounslow's Chief Customs Officer, Mr Phillips. George Stevenson-Reece settled himself into one of the two small seats in the passenger compartment, facing the cargo which had been stowed on the opposite seat, and the hinged canopy covering the passenger compartment was closed and secured by ground staff. The weather was grey and misty as Bill settled himself in the aircraft's open cockpit and prepared for take off. Later he recalled:

"We all knew that a great deal of public opinion depended upon the success or otherwise of this pioneer attempt to operate a regular air service and as pilot of the machine and out of regard to Aircraft Transport and Travel Ltd. (Airco), the operators of the service, I was determined to get through to schedule at all costs.

It was a grim morning, pouring with rain, and with practically no visibility. I had my doubts about being able to make the flight at all, but I knew how keen Sir Sefton Brancker and Mr.Holt-Thomas were to see their Company inaugurate a regular air service, and therefore, inspired by their tremendous enthusiasm, I started off."

"The weather reports in those days were very odd; that is to say, if and when one could obtain a report at all. On this particular day we received the following from the Met. Office at Le Bourget: 'Bolsoms in Channel and squaggy'. Someone remarked: 'Whatever Bolsoms may be, it's about time the minesweepers cleared them all out of the Channel!'"

At 9.10 am Bill lifted G-EAJC off the grass of Hounslow Heath, turning on to a south-easterly heading to fly around the suburbs of south west London heading towards his first check point overhead the military aerodrome at Waddon on the outskirts of Croydon, where he would make a heading change of about 20 degrees to the South towards the next turning point at Edenbridge railway station, where he turned on to an easterly course to follow the prominent railway line marking the route which ran straight as an arrow through Tonbridge and on to Ashford, before heading south-eastwards again towards Folkestone and the English Channel. Bill commented on the problems of navigation in early commercial aircraft:

"After much ado, and considerable difficulties with an insubordinate engine, off we flew. I had a pretty sticky time flying over the outskirts of London, and had to hang on to my compass, which swung about anywhere within 45 degrees."

Bill Lawford in the cockpit of an Airco DH4a

Courtesy of the Flight Collection

Seated in the cramped passenger compartment of the Airco 4A, George Stevenson-Reece described his first aerial view of the English countryside:

"Just after 9 am we started taxiing round the aerodrome. We climbed to 1000 feet and London lay almost invisible to the east, for the radius of vision was not more than four of five miles. As we passed over a suburb seamed with railway lines the altimeter registered 2000 feet. Through a rift in the ground fog the Crystal Palace showed like a child's toy.

Three minutes later we were passing over open country at from 95 to 100 miles an hour and for a moment the Thames appeared like a strip of varnished zinc.

Half an hour aloft and the country looks as if a gigantic steamroller has flattened out every crease of it. Straight ahead the white-fringed line of the Channel is just visible. We are over 4000 feet up and the ant's eggs dotted about the pastures below are sheep."

About 45 minutes after leaving Hounslow they crossed the coast near Folkestone. By now G-EAJC had climbed to an altitude of 5000 feet, which Bill considered a safe height for the Channel crossing in a single engine aircraft which had seen military service. Soon they sighted the French coast near Cap Griz-Nez, and followed it southwards to Boulogne, where the route turned inland towards Abbeville and the river Somme. Memories of the recent conflict were still fresh in Stevenson-Reece's mind:

"Over Boulogne I strain my eyes to catch a glimpse of the old battle region or of familiar landmarks, but the haze hides them all. Etaples is on the right, but there is no sign of life along those miles of coast line that were recently so populous.

Montreuil shoots from under us at 110 miles an hour. The Ecole Militare, home of the G.H.Q. for over two years seems deserted. Abbeville, a mass of lines and huts drops behind and we have done 150 miles in an hour and a half. The Somme marshes glint under the brightening sky. The mist thickens ahead and clears again suddenly as the houses begin to thicken. LeBourget aerodrome stretches in front of us and we start to descend. Yes, Paris was away over on the right but even now it is scarcely visible as a whole owing to the fog. I search in vain for the Eiffel Tower and the Sacre Coeur and try to persuade myself that I like "banking" as we curl downwards to arrive just 2 hours and 20 minutes after leaving Hounslow."

Bill described their arrival at Le Bourget:

"I spotted the Seine, and was soon comfortably bumping down on Le Bourget Aerodrome. Here a hearty welcome awaited us from Mr. Holt-Thomas and other aviation personalities, together with a crowd of reporters and press photographers. What amused me most was the robust old Gendarme, who rushed up and embraced me with 'Allo Mon vieux, 'Allo, Passports s'il vous plait! I had been doing this journey regularly in the RFC and R.A.F., but carried out as a civil flight it was considered quite a feat!"

French Customs examine the freight aboard G-EAJC at Le Bourget

E.H. Lawford archive

The first flight of the regular service to LeBourget had been uneventful apart from the failure of G-EAJC's windmill driven right-hand fuel pump. It had inaugurated Aircraft Transport & Travel's regular service to Paris and was the first flight to be completed between Hounslow and LeBourget under the provisional agreement permitting regular flights between Great Britain and France. George Holt-Thomas knew that this flight marked an important landmark for his company and had absented himself from the first day of the important international conference which he had convened at the Hague to be present at Le Bourget, together with many aviation personalities and the press, to witness the arrival of G-EAJC from Hounslow. At the time great importance was attached to achieving a "First", and as his company had beaten the competion it would generate plenty of publicity for the new service. Bill's logbook entry[5], underlined in red, describes this flight as the "*First Flight of regular Civilian Continental Service*", and for many years it was acknowledged as the first flight of the first regular, daily, sustained scheduled international civil air service for passengers and freight. The word *"regular"* is important as the Company was intent on showing that a regular, reliable, fast air service for both passengers and freight could be operated for the first time. Among the congratulatory telegrams that awaited Bill on his return to Hounslow was one from the House of Commons which read:

"Hearty congratulations and best of luck, did the cream become butter enroute?"
John Clennell

Bill remained at Le Bourget on standby until Wednesday 27th August, but there is some doubt as to the subsequent movements of his passenger George Stevenson-Reece. In a "Late Night Special" edition of that day's "Evening Standard" he reported:

"Hounslow, Monday afternoon, I have just landed back from Paris after having done the journey in five and three quarter hours by air.........."

Whether Stevenson-Reece did fly back to Hounslow that day is uncertain. What is fact however is that a photographer from the art staff of the Paris "Daily Mail", Victor Console, travelled on the only flight to be made from LeBourget to Hounslow that day in the Airco 9b, G-EAGX, piloted by Lieut. "Jim" McMullin. This aircraft could accommodate two passengers in open cockpits, but Aircraft Transport and Travel's Traffic Book[6] shows only one passenger as having travelled from LeBourget to Hounslow. Thus, if Stevenson-Reece did return to Hounslow on this flight, there is a discrepancy. The "Daily Mail" also reported erroneously that Bill travelled back to Hounslow on this flight, but his logbook clearly states that he was *"standing-bye at LeBourget."* It is possible that Stevenson-Reece did fly back to Hounslow with "Jim" McMullin, but it is more likely that he gave the story of his outbound flight to Paris in G-EAJC to Victor Console to carry back to Hounslow in time for

---

[5]See Appendix 2

[6]See Appendix 3

inclusion the late evening editions of his paper, or possibly he filed it by telephone from Paris. Either way, he succeeded in "scooping" his rivals.

The purpose of this flight has been questioned for many years. It may be that the original intention was to operate both the Airco 16, K130, and G-EAJC on the 12:30 departure to provide extra capacity. This happened later in the week when a supplementary aircraft was required to accommodate passengers on the timetabled departure from Hounslow on Friday 29th August, and the planned departure time was brought forward to ensure that A.T.&T. would be the first company to complete a flight from Hounslow to LeBourget that day. It also ensured that George Stevenson-Reece was able to file his report on the new service in time for inclusion in the Late Edition of the London "Evening Standard."

The 12:30 Departure from LeBourget to Hounslow

After completion of arrival formalities at LeBourget, Bill assisted with the preparations for the 12.30pm departure of the Airco 9b, G-EAGX, to Hounslow, piloted by Lieut. C.R."Jim" McMullin. Passengers were accommodated in two open cockpits in the Airco 9b, and a flying helmet, goggles and leather overcoat were provided to give some protection against the cold and the slipstream.

This flight was seen off by George Holt-Thomas and a gathering of French aviation personalities including the French fighter ace, General Gaillard. Many press representatives were present and the departure was filmed by Gaumont. It was reported that McMullin's passenger, Victor Console, had paid 700 francs for his ticket.

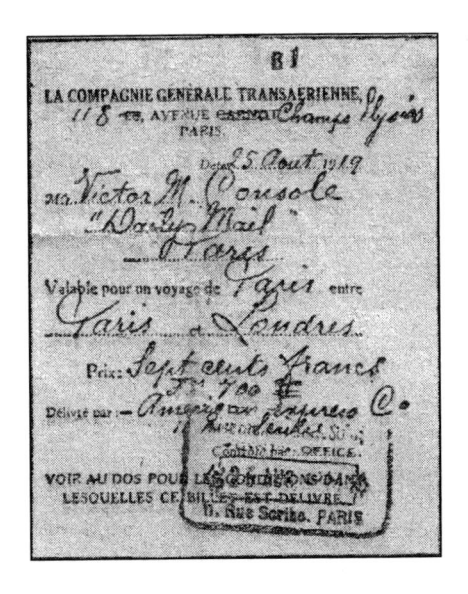

The Ticket
Issued to
Victor Console
by
Aircraft Transport &
Travel's
Paris Agents
La Compagnie General
Transaerienne

Victor Console has his Ticket examined by A.T.&T's Manager at LeBourget, Sydney St. Barbe, prior to boarding G-EAGX. The figure on the left is George Holt-Thomas

      Console carried with him copies of that day's Paris newspapers, letters and "Daily Mail" picture albums of the Paris Peace Conference for presentation to the Lord Mayor of London and the Under Secretary of State for Air, together with a package of valuables for Lloyds Bank. He described his flight from Paris to Hounslow:

"I called at the office of the American Express Company today about 11am and brought my ticket, the first issued. I was soon at the LeBourget aerodrome. There were no formalities. 'Had I anything to declare?' - 'No'. 'Would I take a luncheon basket?' - 'Please".

I donned a flying helmet and on the stroke of 12.30 I was away We rise to 5000 feet and the speed reaches 100 miles per hour. I eat some sandwiches, drink a bottle of beer and smoke a cigarette and there is the Channel beneath and I must drop the bottle in to it. It is very rough, the pilot dives skilfully between the clouds and steadies the machine in the wind gusts. Never are we out of sight of the land, the White Cliffs of Dover are below us and I note that from coast to coast it takes just 10 minutes. I make a few notes and take a photograph or two, and we are over Hounslow. Here I just answer a few questions, sign my name and the journey is over."

Victor Console reported that the flight arrived at 2:46 pm, only one minute behind schedule, but the Traffic Book states that G-EAGX arrived at 2:40 pm. As G-EAGX arrived at Hounslow before the arrival of A.T.&T's scheduled 12:30 pm departure from Hounslow arrived at Le Bourget, it was the first scheduled flight of the service to be completed according to timetable.

The 13:05 Departure from Hounslow to LeBourget

Aircraft Transport and Travel had scheduled a 12:30 pm departure from Hounslow to LeBourget to be operated by the prototype Airco 16, K130, piloted by Major Cyril Patteson, a former C/O of the R.A.F. No. 1 Communications Squadron, who had surveyed the London - Paris route for the Air Ministry as back in 1918. The A.T.&T Traffic Book gives a departure time of 12:40 pm for this flight, but according to one of the passengers, Capt. Bruce Ingram, it was delayed until well after 1:00 pm to await the arrival of the Comptroller General of Civil Aviation, General Sykes, which again brings into question the absolute accuracy of this document. Capt. Ingram stated:

" .....the aeroplane did not start till 35 minutes after schedule time as the coming of Major Sykes, who was to give this new service between the British and French capitals a send off, was delayed."

This flight carried four passengers, including Capt. Ingram, the special representative of the "Illustrated London News", who had been invited by A.T.&T to report on the new service. The identity of the other passengers is not known, but one was an Army Officer and the other two were probably newspaper representatives. The flight was seen off by General Sykes, Brigadier-General Francis Festing, General Manager of A.T.&T, together with many representatives of the local and national press. Major Patteson taxied out in gusty conditions and took off into the low cloud base. His departure was filmed by British Pathe.

The first leg of the flight over southern England and the Channel was relatively smooth and uneventful, but as it crossed the French coast Bruce Ingram reported that the flight encountered bad turbulence:

"It was decidedly bumpy, and this bumping gives the feeling that one experiences when a lift suddenly descends and seems to leave part of one's anatomy behind."

Ingram also described K 130's arrival at Le Bourget:

"And then, almost before we could take it in, we were sailing over a huge aerodrome where were clustered hundreds of German 'planes. In a few minutes we touched ground and were "taxiing" to the hangers, just two hours and twenty minutes from door to door, in spite of an adverse wind."

Mr. Phillips, Chief Customs Officer, checks Major Patteson's papers prior to the departure of K130

There is a discrepancy between the arrival time of 3.05 pm stated in the Traffic Book and the arrival time of 3:30 pm reported in the Daily Mail the following day. If we accept Bruce Ingram's report that this flight did not depart from Hounslow until after 1:00 pm, then the reported arrival time of 3:30 pm is more likely to be correct after a flight lasting 2 hours 25 minutes and the Traffic Book is in error. Although this flight had been delayed, it was the first flight operated from Hounslow to LeBourget according to the company's published timetable which gave a published departure time of 12:30 pm from both Hounslow and LeBourget. Later, at the end of March 1920 after the London terminal had been transferred from Hounslow to Croydon, this flight was dropped in favour of two simultaneous daily departures from Croydon and LeBourget at 9:30 am and 4:30 pm.

Major Cyril Patteson carries out engine checks before departure of K130 from Hounslow, 25th August 1919

A.T.&T's first day of regular operation between Hounslow and LeBourget had achieved three important "firsts" :

09:10   AIRCO 4A, G-EAJC, departed HOUNSLOW 09:10, arrived LeBOURGET 11:30
                Lieut. Lawford with 1 Passenger + mixed freight
                FIRST FLIGHT OF A REGULAR, SUSTAINED, INTERNATIONAL AIR SERVICE TO BE OPERATED FOLLOWING THE REMOVAL OF THE PROHIBITION OF SUCH SERVICES.

12:30   AIRCO 9B, G-EAGX, departed LeBOURGET, arrived HOUNSLOW 14:30
Lieut. McMullin with 1 Passenger + documents
FIRST FLIGHT OPERATED ACCORDING TO TIMETABLE FROM LeBOURGET TO HOUNSLOW AND FIRST SCHEDULED SERVICE TO BE COMPLETED.

c.13:05   AIRCO 16, K130, departed HOUNSLOW, arrived LeBOURGET c.15:25
Major Patteson with 4 Passengers
FIRST FLIGHT OPERATED ACCORDING TO TIMETABLE FROM HOUNSLOW TO LeBOURGET

Passengers disembark from K 130 at Le Bourget, 25th August 1919. Bill Lawford is on the extreme right by the wing tip. Fourth figure from the right is probably George Holt-Thomas.

Tuesday 26th August 1919

Chief Pilot Jerry Shaw's planned 12:30 pm departure in the Airco 4A, G-EAJD, from Hounslow to LeBourget was delayed for 35 minutes, probably due to the continuing spell of unsettled weather. This aircraft carried a full complement of two passengers and some parcels, arriving at LeBourget 2 hours and 20 minutes later after what Shaw described as *"a very bumpy trip in low clouds and rainstorms."*

At LeBourget passengers arriving for the 12:30 pm departure were advised that the weather reports unfavourable with frequent squalls and a strong gale blowing in the Channel and that flying conditions were extremely bumpy. It was reported by Bruce Ingram that in order to demonstrate that the service could operate in all weathers Mr. Holt-Thomas had instructed Major Patteson to depart on time at 12:30 pm. The return flight to Hounslow in the Airco 16, K130, carried 3 passengers, including Major Ingram. All had all decided to brave the turbulent weather which Ingram described thus:

"...at times it was found necessary to rise above the clouds, which were spread out like a vast field of snow below us; another time we entered a terrific squall with driving rain - a magnificent and impressive sight. Across the Channel it was very thick and we had to descend as low as 200 feet at which altitude the major part of the "sea passage" was covered. Then, on reaching the English coast the wind was so strong and it was so bumpy that the pilot had to rise to a considerable height to get relief."

During the flight Major Patteson passed a written note through the small hatch connecting the pilot's open cockpit to the passenger compartment commenting:

"I'm having hell, but we'll get there O.K."

After a over three hours in the air they landed safely at Hounslow. Bruce Ingram remarked that the experience was not as bad as he had expected, and praised the flying skill of Major Patteson, emphasising that A.T.&T. was determined to maintain a reliable service in all weathers.

Wednesday 27th August

The strong winds and poor weather conditions continued, delaying "Jim" McMullin's departure from Hounslow, but he eventually left at 1.43 pm in the Airco 9b, G-EAGX, for LeBourget in an 800 foot cloud base, carrying one passenger and parcels. The return service from LeBourget was flown by Bill Lawford in G-EAJC, carrying two passengers, Lieut. Fryer and Lady Muriel Paget, the first lady passenger to be carried on the service. Bill described this flight as *"extremely bumpy"* and he was forced to climb to 12,000 feet to get on top of the weather, battling against a strong headwind, reaching Hounslow after a 3 hour 10 minute flight. During the flight 'JC's right hand petrol pump failed yet again.

Thursday 28th August

The gales now increased to storm force, with torrential rain and a reported cloud base of only 100 feet, forcing the cancellation of the outward service from Hounslow. Bill described conditions as *"awful weather and gales 99 mph,"*

Lieut Henry "Jerry" Shaw, Chief Pilot, Airco and Aircraft Transport and Travel Ltd

Courtesy of the Flight Collection

Nevertheless, at LeBourget Jerry Shaw decided to brave the storm-force south-westerly winds and leave for Hounslow in in the Airco 4A G-EAJD. He took off on schedule carrying two passengers, an American businessman and an Irish priest. So turbulent was the flight that that the two passengers were convinced that their pilot was enjoying himself by performing "stunts", so they calmed their nerves by downing a bottle of brandy. Shaw noted in his log:

"it was a terrible trip. Hurricane 100 mph blowing from S.W., heavy rain and clouds, 400 ft. in England."

Approaching the English coast Shaw decided that he had had enough and decided to land at Lympne. However, as he circled the aerodrome he saw one of the canvas Bessoneau hangers picked up by the wind and blown across the airfield, so he elected to continue on to Hounslow. The authorities at Lympne alerted Hounslow that Shaw was on his way, and a landing party was hastily assembled to assist him after touchdown. As Shaw landed into the gale his groundspeed was virtually nil, but the aircraft was firmly caught by three men at each wing tip and walked to the shelter of the hangers. Shaw was offered the remains of the brandy bottle by his relieved passengers, one of whom had tested the strength of the cabin roof with his head and emerged from the aircraft with the rim of his bowler hat around his neck. The flight had been completed in a record time of 1 hour 55 minutes. Congratulations on completing the flight in such atrocious conditions were received by the company from the C.G.C.A, Gen.Sykes, but the Airco 4A had to be withdrawn from service for complete re-rigging and was grounded for three days.

Friday 29th August

By Friday morning the gales were slowly abating. Conditions over England remained poor with low clouds, rain and a gusty wind, but in France the weather was improving and three flights were operated from Hounslow to LeBourget. At 8:58 am an Airco 4A, piloted by Capt. Alan Riley, left Hounslow carrying two passengers who had been delayed by the cancellation of the previous day's service to LeBourget.

At 12:30 pm Bill departed on time with the regular service flying the Airco 16, which now carried it's permanent registration letters G-EACT, replacing the temporary registration markings, K130. His four passengers were Sir Sydney Lea, Mr.A.H. Davies and Mr.& Mrs. Leonard Aldridge. This was the busiest day of the week, and a supplementary flight was operated to LeBourget by Capt. Baylis, who departed from Hounslow shortly after Bill in an Airco 9b with two extra passengers and some parcels.

Only one aircraft left LeBourget for Hounslow, an Airco 9b flown by "Jim" McMullin operating the regular service carrying 2 passengers and parcels, but the continuing poor weather conditions over England forced him to make an unscheduled landing at Kenley at 3 pm, from where his passengers and cargo continued their journey to London by road.

Saturday 30th August

Saturday saw a further moderation in the weather conditions, with broken cloud and a light north westerly wind. "Jim" McMullin positioned the Airco 9b from Kenley to Hounslow following his forced landing, arriving at 10:15 am. The regular service to LeBourget was operated by an Airco 4A, piloted by Capt. Gerald Gathergood, who left on time carrying 2 passengers. Two flights operated from LeBourget to Hounslow. Capt Riley left in an Airco 4A with two passengers and parcels, arriving at 3:20 pm, followed by an additional flight flown by Capt Baylis in an Airco 9b carrying one passenger and parcels, which included an urgent consignment of millinery for a leading West End store.

This may be the 8.58 departure from Hounslow on Friday 29th August which was delayed from the previous day by the storm. The figure wearing a leather greatcoat in the foreground may be Capt. Alan Riley receiving clearance from Mr. Phillips, Chief Customs Officer at Hounslow.

The AJ Jackson Collection at Brooklands Museum

Three Aircraft Transport and Travel aircraft at Hounslow, August 1919

The A.J.Jackson Collection at Brooklands Museum

So ended the first week's operation of A.T.&T's London - Paris service during which only one flight was cancelled because of weather conditions. Aircraft Transport and Travel had demonstrated that a reliable civil air service could be operated between the two capitals.

Pioneer Airline Pilot

Following the first week of operations weather conditions improved and little disruption occurred to the London – Paris service until the following November. On 2nd September the A.T.&T. lost it's monopoly position on the route when Handley-Page Air Transport commenced a thrice weekly service between Hounslow and LeBourget with their twin engined H.P. 0/7 airliners. These were civilianised versions of the 0/400 bomber which could carry up to 14 passengers in the comfort of a spacious enclosed cabin. Handley-Page promoted the extra safety of their twin-engined machines and offered lower fares than their rival, A.T.&T, but omitted to mention that in the event of one engine failing a forced landing would be inevitable as the H.P. 0/7 was unable to maintain height with one engine inoperative. The H.P. 0/7 was also slower than A.T.&T's single engined aircraft and the Company countered Handley-Page's publicity by promoting the higher speed of their fleet, styling their service as the "Air Express."

During mid-September A.T.&T.'s French associate, the "Compagnie General Transaeriennes" (C.G.T.) began operations on the route using the three seat Breguet 14 aircraft, and the close association between the two companies was emphasised when the C.G.T. logo was carried on the port fuselage side of A.T.&T's Airco 16, G-EACT, for a short period.

The Airco 16, G-EACT carrying the name of the French Company C.G.T.

E.H. Lawford Archive

Only five pilots, Lawford, Shaw, Riley, McMullin and Baylis regularly flew on the daily A.T.&T. service during the first three weeks of operation, and all were employed through Airco, A.T.&T's parent company. Shaw, together with Gathergood and possibly Patteson, who rarely flew on the regular service, were also kept busy carrying out test, delivery, and demonstration flights for Airco.

On the 1st September the Airco 4A, G-EAJD, returned to service following extensive checks and re-rigging after Jerry Shaw's eventful flight at the height of the previous week's storms from LeBourget to Hounslow, and was flown on the regular service to LeBourget by Shaw.

The international press continued to report favourably on the new service. In early September a representative of the "New York Times" reported 5his experiences on a flight from LeBourget to Hounslow with Bill Lawford. It was usual for the pilots to accede to special requests from their passengers whenever possible, and in excellent visibility he requested Bill to climb up to 10,000 feet to obtain a panoramic view of south east England and the English Channel.

The second Airco 16, G-EALM, had now been completed and on 9th September "Jerry" Shaw made a final test flight at Hendon before delivering the aircraft to A.T.&T. at Hounslow. Three days later Bill flew this aircraft on its maiden trip to LeBourget with four passengers.

Aircraft Transport and Travel's second Airco 16, G-EALM

Hillyer Collection, via Albert E. Smith and Croydon Airport Society

No. 1 Communications Squadron, R.A.F, had been disbanded on 30th September, and A.T.&T. was occasionally called upon to operate special V.I.P. flights on behalf of the Government. This made sense as most A.T.&T's pilots had previously served with the Communications Squadrons and and were personally known to senior politicians and civil servants. Jerry Shaw was called to make a special flight at short notice during the late afternoon of 9th September from Hounslow to LeBourget in the Airco 16, G-EACT, with the Controller General of Civil Aviation, General Sykes, and the Under Secretary of State for Air, Major General Seeley. His passengers had been summoned to Paris at for urgent discussions in connection with the finalisation of the I.C.A.N. Regulations, which were to be approved the following day. Sea fog blanketed the English Channel, but the land areas were clear, and Shaw flew above the fog-covered Channel, arriving at Le Bourget for an overnight stop. The following day he left for the coastal resort of Deauville with his two passengers, who were to meet the Prime Minister David Lloyd George for discussions in connection with the International Conference on the Middle East. Reaching Les Andelys Shaw found that the extensive Channel fog still covered the area, and after a fruitless search for a suitable landing field General Seeley ordered Shaw to return to LeBourget. By the following day the fog had cleared and Shaw left LeBourget once more for Deauville, landing in a small field near Cabourg, where his two passengers disembarked to meet with Lloyd-George. It was late when they returned, and Shaw did not arrive back at LeBourget until well after dusk. Gen. Sykes flew returned to London with Shaw the following morning.

By mid September the weather was again testing the skills of the pilots. Flying from LeBourget on the 15th Bill recorded:

"above clouds at 4000', most of the way at 500' to 1500', a very bad trip - crossed Channel at about 500' - compass course most of the way."

Crossing in the opposite direction "Jerry" Shaw noted:

"Low clouds and poor visibility - very bad in places. Engine popping."

The pilots flew in all but the worst weather conditions, and the service was now gaining a reputation for reliability. At the end of the third week's operation on the London - Paris route it was estimated that the company's aircraft had flown 10,000 revenue miles and that 41 out of a possible 42 flights had been completed successfully, with only one forced landing.

On 18th September Jerry Shaw delivered the third Airco 16, G-EALU, from the Airco works at Hendon to at Hounslow for A.T.&T, followed on the 20th by the Airco 4A, G-EAHG, which had recently returned from the E.L.T.A. Exhibition at Amsterdam. This aircraft did not remain at Hounslow for long as

Airco 4a, G-EAHG, photographed at Innsbruck, Switzerland, during Major Stewart-Wortley's Sales Tour. An external pannier for carrying skis is visible on the side of the fuselage

The A.J. Jackson Collection at Brooklands Museum

the Swiss government had shown considerable interest in Airco's products and consequently on 24th September Major Stewart-Wortley, Airco's newly appointed Sales Representative, departed with G-EAHG on a sales tour of Switzerland.

During the second half of September the A.T.&T. pilot strength was increased and six new pilots joined the company. These were Mr. Square, George Powell, Alan Campbell-Orde, H.W. Chattaway and Frank Courtney. On the 24th September A.T.&T. completed a month of operation on the London-Paris service. The company had flown an estimated 13,750 revenue miles and completed 54 flights out of a possible 56, and these figures were well publicised to underline the reliability of the service. Bill had logged a total of 31 hours flying during the first four weeks of the service, for which he received extra flying pay of £18-12s-2d. George Holt-Thomas paid tribute to the pilots who had flown on the service during the first month's operation:

"To the pioneers of commercial flying, to Captains Baylis and Riley, Lieutenants Shaw, Lawford, and McMullin, we owe a debt of gratitude it is hard to express in words. Their flying, their enthusiasm, their good judgement - these have been magnificent"

As a token of his appreciation Holt-Thomas presented each pilot with a 22 carat gold cigarette case carrying the inscription:

> *"In appreciation of the first month of the London Paris service,*
> *G. Holt Thomas."*

With the Paris service now well established, A.T.&T planned to open new routes and Bill was sent to Holland on behalf of the Company to locate suitable landing grounds. He travelled to Holland by rail and boat spending ten days surveying possible sites at Rotterdam, The Hague, and Utrecht, all of which were later to become established aerodromes. On his return he spent time at Airco's Hendon office and at Hounslow writing reports on his Dutch trip[7]. This was the first of a series of steps which would lead to A.T&T's association with the new Dutch airline company K.L.M., which had been formed in Amsterdam on 7th October 1919.

Bill returned to flying duties on 10th October and demonstrated the Airco 4A, G-EAJD, to a representative of the Spanish Government. On the 16th he flew a group of Norwegians to Paris and was invited to join them for a social evening at Maxims. The flight from London had been extremely bumpy, and one Bill's passengers, Mr Halvorsen, wrote what must be one of the earliest endorsements by an airline passenger:

> *"My wife and I returned to our home on Sunday and had a very good crossing of the North Sea. We will always remember with the greatest pleasure the splendid flight from London to Paris, and the charming and excellent gentleman who piloted us down."*

Also that day Capt. Gerald Gathergood made a special flight carrying urgent mail from Hounslow to LeBourget in a record time of only 80 minutes flying the Airco 9R, G-EAHT, at an average groundspeed of 180 mph. The following week Gathergood broke 18 British records for closed circuit flight flying this aircraft. Later in the month Bill was filmed from an Airco 9 camera aircraft by Pathe News flying the Airco 16, G-EACT, on the regular service to Paris.

A national rail strike at the end of September resulted in extra business for both Airco and A.T.&T. aircraft when the twin engine Airco 10 light bomber, G-EAJO, was chartered by the Post Office to fly mail between Hendon and Glasgow. But intensive aircraft utilisation was now beginning to tell on the A.T.&T. fleet, many of which had seen military service before being converted

---

[7]See Appendix 5, Page 2

for civil use. Jerry Shaw was ferrying the Airco 4A, G-EAJC, from Hounslow to Hendon for a top overhaul of the engine when a section of the exhaust pipe fell off the aircraft. On the 13th Capt. Baylis, flying an Airco 16 from LeBourget to Hounslow, was forced to make an emergency landing in northern France near Grandvilliers with a broken propellor reduction gear. The aircraft had to be dismantled and was transported by road to LeBourget.

Later in the month an unreliable compass resulted in Bill having to force land more than 50 miles to the east of Paris in the Airco 4A, G-EAHF:

" Hounslow to Paris, forced landed at Ferte Gaucher, down to 400 feet in thick fog at Grandvillers - engine knocking and popping badly - compass totally dud, points south for east which took me off my course and landed me east of Paris. Put machine, which was O.K,. in military French hangar and went with passenger by train to Paris."

The following day Bill returned to Ferte Gaucher with two Airco mechanics and 'HF was ferried to LeBourget for a thorough check over. The weather remained unsettled, and on the 28th he departed from LeBourget with 'HF on the regular flight to Hounslow with one passenger. But the aircraft still had problems:

"Le Bourget to Hounslow, compass totally wrong, engine popping and vibrating, vile weather down to 500 feet most of the way, very strong headwind, visibility nil."

Bill arrived safely at Hounslow, but Jerry Shaw was not so fortunate when he experienced a similar problem with the Airco 4A, G-EAHG, which had now returned from the sales tour of Switzerland. Shaw flew the outbound service to Le Bourget with 'HG on 27th October, and had reported *"compass dud and throttle loose."* On the 29th he left LeBourget for Hounslow in 'HG carrying a single passenger, Mr. Oelrichs. The weather was very poor and after spending some time flying low over the Channel with an unreliable compass Shaw soon became lost in the low cloud and mist. Uncertain of his position he climbed up into cloud, hoping to break out above the cloud layer and obtain a bearing from the sun, but with no blind flying instruments he soon stalled and began an uncontrolled descent, only regaining control of the aircraft just above the sea. With fuel now running low Shaw was lucky to spot a small coaster, the "Harlech", in the misty conditions, and decided to ditch alongside the ship. Realising Shaw's intentions his passenger, Mr. Oelrichs, removed some of his clothing in preparation for the ditching, and pulled his bowler hat firmly down on to his head in the hope that it would act as a crash helmet. Shaw made a

Advertisment for the Airco 16 aircraft published during December 1919

textbook ditching, and the aircraft remained afloat for some time as it was equipped with flotation bags. The rim of Oelrich's bowler hat was now wedged round his neck, and Shaw helped him on to the aircraft's wing before returning to the passenger compartment to retrieve the cargo of parcels. None the worse for their experience, the two men were taken aboard the "Harlech", which continued on it's voyage, leaving the aircraft to disappear beneath the waves. Next day Shaw and his passenger were put ashore at Weymouth. After obtaining Customs clearance for the cargo of parcels Shaw sent a tongue-in-cheek telegram to A.T.&T. at Hounslow - *"Landed at Weymouth, proceeding to Waterloo."*

Despite growing reliability problems and the onset of the autumn weather it was estimated that at the end of October, following nine weeks of regular operations on the London - Paris route, that A.T.&T. had flown a total of 34,000 revenue miles. On an estimated 37 out of a possible 54 days the weather had been considered unfavourable for flying, but nevertheless 135 out of 139 scheduled flights had been completed. To promote the company's image as the "Air Express" it was emphasised that an average speed of 106 mph had been achieved by the Company's aircraft on the route, a higher figure than that of the rival Handley Page Air Transport. A further two Airco 9b's, G-EAOP and 'OZ had now been added to the fleet and more pilots had also been recruited, including Lieuts. Armstrong, Lindley, Tebbit, Robins and Game.

A.T.&T.'s record of reliability had now satisfied the Post Office authorities that an Air Mail service between London and Paris was viable, and in early November it was announced by the Postmaster General that A.T.&T. had been awarded an initial six month contract to provide an Air Mail service to Paris, guaranteeing a same day delivery to the French capital. The new service was to begin on 10th November, with a surcharge of 2s 6d (12.5p) an ounce payable for each letter. A special fleet of motorcycles equipped with sidecars would collect the Air Mail from eight designated Post Offices in the London area and convey it to Hounslow, where it would be loaded on board a special Airco 4A flying a special "Royal Mail" pennant attached to the aircraft's rudder. The inaugural Air Mail flight was scheduled for the 10th November, but was aborted when the pilot, "Jim" McMullen, was forced to return to Hounslow shortly after take-off due to low cloud and poor visibility, and it was not until the following day that Capt. Baylis completed the first Air Mail flight to LeBourget in Airco 4A, G-EAHF.

During early November Bill was busy working on plans for the planned new service to Amsterdam, but the onset of winter and the reluctance of the Dutch government to sign up to the I.C.A.N. Agreement meant that the start of the new service was postponed until the following spring. On 12th November in cold and foggy weather, Bill made his first Air Mail flight to Paris. The turn of the season and increasing serviceability problems with the A.T.&T. fleet caused serious disruption during November and December 1919. The difficulties faced by the small band of pioneer airline pilots were underlined by two incidents caused by bad weather and mechanical problems during this period. On 22nd November, after delaying for an hour, Bill left Hounslow flying an Airco 4A with two passengers on the daily service to LeBourget. After crossing the Channel at very low altitude he was forced down by cloud and poor visibility at Les Barracks near Calais, not far from the spot where Louis Bleriot had taken off in 1909 to make the first flight by aeroplane across the English Channel :

"Hounslow to Paris, forced landing at Les Barracks near Calais owing to clouds and rain nearly touching the ground - a most alarming and dangerous experience - nearly crashed into the cliffs at Griz Nez, at 50 feet over Channel, however landed O.K."

Bill put his two passengers on the train to Paris and waited for the weather to clear. Next day he took-off for Hounslow, landing en-route at the emergency aerodrome at Penshurst for fuel, but as none was available he was forced to fly on to Kenley to re-fuel before continuing on his flight to Hounslow. A few days later, on 27th November, Lieut.George Powell was also forced to divert to Penshurst due to fog at Hounslow, and by mid-January 1920 Penshurst had been officially recognised as a diversionary aerodrome.

One of the special fleet of motorcycles with sidecars used to bring Air Mail from London Post Offices to Hounslow Aerodrome
Courtesy of the Flight Collection

The following week, after crossing the Channel en-route to Paris with two passengers and mails in the Airco 4A, G-EAHF, Bill was forced down at Wimereux:

"Forced landing due to base plugs of carburettor float chamber unscrewing and getting lost in air, causing engine stoppage."

He spent the next four days checking the security of the aircraft which he had hurriedly tied down to ride out the stormy weather while awaiting the arrival of a mechanic from Airco:

"Having a dreadful time with machine pegged out in open, exposed to gales etc. Wet through several times daily."

Five days elapsed before Bill got airborne during the afternoon in 'HF with an Airco mechanic, Mr. New. It took 50 minutes to cross the Channel flying against a strong headwind, and they spent the night at Lympne Aerodrome before continuing on to Hounslow next morning. It had been a week since Bill had left Hounslow for LeBourget.

Incidents like these were a part of everyday life for the early airline pilots, and together with the many hours spent flying in unheated open cockpits in all weathers, they were beginning to take their toll. A week later Bill attended a Medical Board for his routine 6 monthly medical check and was advised to take 3 months off as he was "run down".

There were problems due to the lack of permanent Customs facilities at the important diversionary aerodrome of Lympne. Major Patteson was forced to land there on 28th November due to bad weather and low fuel en-route from LeBourget to Hounslow with four passengers in the Airco 16, G-EACT. The nearest Customs office at Folkestone was immediately notified of his unscheduled arrival, but the passengers were anxious to continue their journey without delay and as no Customs Officer was available to attend at Lympne they soon left by road after the Air Ministry C.A.T.O. had obtained their written Customs declarations. H.M.Customs quickly expressed their displeasure, maintaining that the passengers should have remained at the aerodrome until a they could attend, but A.T.&T. countered by claiming that this was unreasonable, and demanded full time Customs attendance at Lympne. The stalemate continued until mid-February 1920 when H.M.Customs relented and agreed to provide a full time presence at the aerodrome.

December 1919 was a bad month for Britain's first international airline. On 11th Lieut. Bradley, inbound on the regular service from Paris in the Airco 4A, G-EAHF, crashed on approach to Kenley while attempting to land in misty conditions. Bradley had been unable to clear the cloud covered North Downs, and was observed flying at an estimated height of only 80 feet above ground.

Visibility at the time was estimated at just 120 yards and Bradley was attempting to land at Kenley when the aircraft struck the top of a tree on Coulsdon Common, a mile from the aerodrome. The crash killed the only passenger aboard the aircraft, an American Banker, Mr George F. Rand, who was returning to London following a meeting with the French Premier, M. Clemanceau. Lieut. Bradley succumbed to his injuries the following day. These were the first fatalities to occur on a British scheduled service. The Airco 4A, G-EAHF, had flown only 107 hours since entering service, and Lieut. Bradley, a popular and experienced pilot with over 1000 hours flying experience, had only recently joined A.T.&T, completing three return flights between London and Paris prior to the crash. The official Report into the accident published by the Air Ministry nine days later found that:

> *"The accident was due to the starboard planes of the machine striking a tree, which the pilot had failed to observe while manoeuvring to land in misty weather."*

The Report also pointed out that the accident underlined the dangers of flying in bad weather, stating that the knowledge and experience of the pilot was not always sufficient to guarantee the safety of a flight made in poor weather conditions. It also recommended that a system of air/ground radio communications should be set up to provide up-to-date meteorological information for the landing grounds along the route. At the inquest into the death of the passenger, Mr. Rand, the solicitor representing A.T.&T. pointed out that had the facilities promised by the Air Ministry at the Penshurst emergency landing ground been available, Lieut. Bradley could have elected to land there instead of continuing on towards the mist covered Kenley Aerodrome with fatal consequences.

The publicity surrounding this accident raised doubts about the safety of flying during the winter months and soon resulted in a downturn in passenger numbers, which prompted A.T.&T. to concentrate on promoting the advantages of it's fast Mail and Parcels Service[8] between the two capitals, a forerunner of the present small package services which now operate globally.

The winter weather caused serious disruption to the service during the month. No flights were operated on the London - Paris route between 12th and 18th of December, and the service was also grounded by fog on 20th, 29th and 30th of the month. By early January A.T.&T.'s previously good record for reliability had been severely dented as only 200 out of the 272 flights scheduled since the start of the service in August had been completed. Airco announced that a new eight passenger aircraft, the Airco 18, powered by a 450 hp Napier

---

[8]See Appendix 5, Page 3

Lion engine and capable of carrying a ton of mail on the European routes, was under construction, and during the month three more Airco 9b's joined A.T.&T's fleet. The loss of the two Airco 4A's G-EAHF and 'HG was made up with the delivery of two more Airco 16's, G-EAPM and 'PT.

Airco 4a, G-EAJD at Hounslow
The A.J. Jackson Collection at Brooklands Museum

    As a result of the recommendations contained in the Air Ministry Report into the accident to G-EAHF at Kenley, there were plans to provide up to date information on flight progress with the installation of radio telephone equipment on the roof of the Company's London office at Buckingham Gate. This equipment could receive up to date information from each aircraft on the route, including it's position, which would be displayed by small model aircraft affixed to a map of the London – Paris route. The new radio equipment was successfully air tested by Jerry Shaw during January 1920 in the Airco 16, G-EALU, after an initial setback when the trailing aerial became entangled with the aircraft during a test flight.

    At Hendon aerodrome Airco were now facing financial problems. George Holt-Thomas's long campaign for Government subsidies to be paid to the airlines had been unsuccessful, and the intensive campaign to market Airco products abroad had met with only limited success. He had begun discussions with the Persian Foreign Minister to acquire the monopoly for domestic air services in Persia, but this project had been dropped at the end of March 1920.

The seasonal downturn of business had reduced A.T.&T.'s requirement for more Airco aircraft, and George Holt-Thomas outlined these problems and proposed a possible solution when he addressed the British Chambers of Commerce at a luncheon in late January:

"The apathy of the Government is destroying our lead.....if a load of 400 lbs/day was guaranteed, Aircraft Transport and Travel could carry it at four shillings per lb, or a penny per letter."

In an attempt to generate new business for Airco "Jim" McMullen departed on a sales tour of Poland and Czechoslovakia at the end of January with the Airco 9b, G-EAPU, "Acanthus". After routeing via Brussels and Berlin, he was forced to land in a German field with engine trouble. This field was surrounded by telephone wires making it dangerous to attempt a take-off, but McMullen negotiated with the local authorities and succeeded in securing the removal of a section of the telephone wires for a payment of only 15 shillings (75p) in German Marks, and he was able to continued on his journey with minimum delay.

Airco 9b, G-EAOZ, with the Napier Lion powered Airco 16, G-EAQS, pictured at Croydon. Note the the three open cockpits of the Airco 9b and the petrol cans in the foreground, used for refuelling before the introduction of fuel pumps and bowsers
The A.J.Jackson Collection Collection at Brooklands Museum

March 1920 would prove to be even more pivotal to the future survival of the A.T.&T. than the setbacks of the previous December, and a chain of events started which would lead to the eventual failure of the company at the end of the year. The operational subsidies provided by foreign governments to their national airlines allowed them to undercut the fares charged by their unsubsidised British competitors and frequent requests from the British airlines for similar subsidies had been ignored by an apathetic government. The matter came to a head in Parliament during the Air Estimates Debate in early March, when the Secretary for War and Air, Winston Churchill, made a shortsighted statement outlining Government policy:

"Civil aviation must fly by itself, the Government cannot possible hold it up in the air."

With an unsympathetic govenment and declining business, George Holt-Thomas resigned as Chairman of A.T.&T and disposed of his controlling interest in A.T.&T.'s parent company, Airco, to the Birmingham Small Arms Company Ltd. Sir Sefton Brancker summed up the situation stating that the Government had been very slow to respond to the situation. He believed that Airco might have survived alone had there been even modest Government help and that the Company could have been in profit within a year. He also pointed out that the airlines could not be expected to rely on cheaply converted war surplus aircraft, observing:

"It is impossible to continue to live on scrap indefinitely."

The new owners of Airco had purchased the company to acquire it's large factory premises at The Hyde, Hendon, and had little interest in continuing the company's aviation activities, but agreed that A.T.&T. could continue flying operations for a further six months, and that Sir Sefton Brancker would stay on as Managing Director for the summer of 1920. Some years later, after Brancker's untimely death in the R.101 disaster, Bill recalled his leadership through these difficult times[9]:

"One could enlarge ad-lib on the enthusiasm of the staff of A.T.&T. from the highest to the lowest - and the highest, General Branker, had that magnetic personality which he radiated to all, revealing himself at once as a great chief and friend. After any particularily nasty flight there was always awaiting his great hearty grip of the hand with a twinkling 'Well done - Cheerio

---

[9] "Sir Sefton Brancker", by Norman McMillan, published by Heinemann, 1935

and stick it old lad,' or a polite little note to that effect, some of which I still have and treasure.

His great secret was that he was human and showed appreciation for those who worked for him, and as a natural result he received one hundred percent unswerving loyalty and affection in return."

Early in March the Air Ministry announced that Hounslow Aerodrome would be withdrawn from use as the London Terminal Aerodrome from 28th March 1920, and replaced by the R.A.F. Aerodrome at Waddon, near Croydon. As the new Terminal was situated to the south of the capital aircraft would no longer have fly over or around the London suburbs before setting course towards the Continent. It was also thought that Waddon was less prone to fog. Early in February 1920 Bill returned to flying duties following a two months break. He echoed the happy-go-lucky atmosphere that prevailed amongst the pilots of the early airlines when a flight to Paris carrying mail and freight in the Airco 9b, G-EAOZ, ended with a bump:

" Hit a hummock and ditch on aerodrome which spoiled a good landing and wiped off the undercarriage - Hard Luck."

Even though the worst of the winter weather had now abated, flights were still occasionally disrupted. Bill described a particularily difficult flight over the Channel:

"Vile mists at Kenley, crossed Channel but unable to land due to mist and fog at Gris Nez. Followed coast past Boulogne, but had to return owing to impossibility of landing - finally landed at Lympne after one hour crossing and re-crossing the Channel."

The French Railways were paralyised by strike action during March 1920 and this resulted in welcome extra business for A.T.&T. when the British newspapers switched their French distribution network from the railways to air freight to ensure distribution during the strike. Seeking further business, A.T.&T. announced that the Company's Hire Department could immediately quadruple the number of aircraft available for freight, passenger and ad-hoc charter work.

The first of the new Napier Lion powered Airco 16's, G-EAQS, had now entered service and made it's first flight on the London - Paris route on 1st March flown by Frank Courtney. The Company's fleet of Airco 16's now totalled seven, but on the 18th March the prototype Airco 16, G-EACT, was lost when Lieut. Harold Game ran out of fuel and ditched in the Channel off Brighton. The aircraft, had left LeBourget at 11.45 that morning for Hounslow carrying a cargo of small packages, and it eventually dissappeared beneath the waves, but luckily Game was rescued by the steamer "Silarnus", en-route from London to Swansea, where he was put ashore a few days later. On the evening of Hounslow's last day as the London Terminal Aerodrome, Bill made a special flight with a "Sunday Times" correspondent, Major W.T. Blake, to report from the air on the annual Oxford and Cambridge Boat Race. From their lofty position above the Race it proved impossible to identify the winners, nevertheless they celebrated the finish by performing some aerobatics. An exhilarated Major Blake reported:

"Up went the nose of the old bus, a DH9, and down went her tail. Somebody had won the Race so we threw a few wild stunts for the benefit of anyone who was watching us."

Over the weekend of the 27th and 28th March 1920 A.T.&T. re-located operations to the new Terminal at Waddon Aerodrome. Ground facilities at Waddon, like those at Hounslow, consisted of the ex-military barracks and hangars recently vacated by the R.A.F. The aerodrome was now officially known as Croydon Airport, and had been formed from two adjoining R.A.F. aerodromes, Beddington to the west and Waddon to the east, separated by a public road, Plough Lane. Storage and maintenance hangars were located on the Beddington side of Plough Lane, and Waddon provided passenger facilities and a small wooden control tower. Movement of aircraft between the two aerodromes was via a gated level crossing over Plough Lane. The landing area was quite rough and very uneven in places and there was a noticeable ridge where the foundations of an old Roman road crossed the site. Bill was no stranger to Waddon as he had flown there during his time with the R.A.F. Communications Squadrons, and he made his first flight from the new Airport on 31st March piloting the daily service to LeBourget. A lack of bookings forced A.T.&T. to suspend the regular service to Paris during the four days of Easter 1920, underlining the company's reliance on the the business community and the very wealthy for it's revenue.

At the end of April, the prototype Airco 18, G-EARI, arrived at Croydon for flight testing. This aircraft had been specifically designed for operations on the London - Paris route, but the type's early operational history is unclear and it is unlikely to have entered service before the issue of it's C.of A. in July. This aircraft had a brief operational career and was written-off on 16th August after the engine lost power and it crashed at Wallington with six passengers aboard.

Early in May the Post Office announced that A.T.&T. had lost the contract to carry Air Mail on the London - Paris Route, and that it had been awarded to A.T.&T's competitor, Handley-Page Air Transport Ltd. This was a serious blow for A.T.&T, the Company had re-tendered for the six monthly contract but had sought increased charges. In an attempt to increase passenger

Major Blake and Bill climb aboard G-EAOZ to Report on the 1920 Oxford and Cambridge Boat Race.
E.H. Lawford Archive

"Contact", starting G-EAOZ for the Boat Race Flight.
E.H. Lawford Archive

SPEED
& SAFETY

AIRCO 18

THE AIRCO 18 has been designed and built especially for COMMERCIAL purposes—to carry either passengers or freight—upon the actual experience gained on the London-Paris route, and is an EMBODIMENT OF THE ENTIRE MILITARY, COMMERCIAL AND SCIENTIFIC EXPERIENCE OF THE DAY.

The machine is fitted with a 450 H.P. NAPIER "LION" ENGINE, and has a speed of 114 m.p.h. and an endurance of 370 miles.

The EIGHT PASSENGERS are accommodated in a very comfortable saloon, and the pilot, seated above and behind the saloon, commands an excellent view for all purposes.

When used for freight this machine carries OVER 2,000 LBS. OF GOODS IN 255 CUBIC FEET

THE AIRCRAFT M^{FG} C^O L^{TD}
THE HYDE   HENDON N.W.9

Advertisement for the new Airco 18

"Aeroplane"

numbers and to compete with the subsidised French airlines now offering a single fare to Paris of £6 - 6 - 0, A.T.&T. now reduced their single fare to £12, and introduced a new timetable with simultaneous departures from both Croydon and LeBourget at 9.30 am and 4.30 pm daily, excepting Sundays. The way was now clear for the start of air services to Holland as the four dissenting countries, Norway, Sweden, Denmark and Holland had agreed to implement the I.C.A.N. Convention following a derogation which allowed German civil aircraft to use their airspace and guaranteed reciprocal transit rights on the direct route to southern Europe through German Airspace to the Dutch colonies in the Far East. The Dutch airline company, Koninklijke Luchtvaart Maatschappij, KLM, headed by Albert Plesman, was now ready to start a service between Amsterdam and London. Plesman was impressed by the standard of A.T.&T's London - Paris service, leading to his decision to charter aircraft from A.T.&T. for the new Amsterdam service before committing to the purchase of aircraft for the new airline.

The inaugural service operated by A.T.&T. on behalf of KLM left Croydon for Amsterdam at 11 am on 17th May, flown by Jerry Shaw in the Airco 16, G-EALU, carrying two journalists, Mr. O'Brien and Mr. Rhodes, a consignment of London newspapers, and a message from the Lord Mayor of London to the Burgomeister of Amsterdam, arriving at Schipol Aerodrome two and a half hours later. Shaw flew the return service to London next day carrying the two British journalists and also the first Dutchman to use the service, Mr. J. Van den Biggelaar, who carried greetings for the Lord Mayor of London and a consignment of Dutch newspapers. The service was timetabled to leave Croydon on Monday, Wednesday and Friday at 10 am, returning from Amsterdam at 11 am on Tuesday, Thursday and Saturday, with a single fare of £15-5-0 and a rate of 2/6 per lb. for small parcels. An onwards connection was available to The Hague and Rotterdam. The flight routed over Calais, Dunkirk, Nieuport, Ostend and The Hague, and it was emphasised that passengers would get an excellent view of the Belgian battlefields and the German heavy gun emplacements enroute, but no reference was made to the vagaries of the weather in the area. On 29th May the first return charter flight from Amsterdam to London in a day was completed when a Dutch business man flew to an urgent meeting in London in the Airco 9b, G-EAGX, and returned home that evening.

Bill took off for Amsterdam on 12th July with one passenger in the Airco 16, G-EALM, but after reaching the Channel he was forced to turn back to Lympne with a failing engine. It was found that a carbon brush was missing from one of the magnetos and that a terminal had become loose. Following repairs he set out again for Amsterdam, but the engine continued to give problems and he only just scraped into Schipol Aerodrome on a very rough running engine. After repairs and a flight test he left for Croydon next day, but the engine continued to misfire and he was forced to land at Lympne before continuing on to Croydon where it was found that a carburettor float was punctured. Among the passengers on this flight was KLM's Managing Director, Albert Plesman, who was travelling to England to finalise the purchase of KLM's first two aircraft, the Airco 9b's G-EAOZ and G-EAPL from A.T.&T. These aircraft were sold to KLM as H-NABF and H-NABE.

A.T.&T. continued to operate the Amsterdam service on behalf of KLM until the end of September 1920, when Plesman wisely decided to suspend operations before the onset of winter. During five months of operation on behalf of KLM, A.T.&T. had carried 345 passengers and a large number of small parcels on the route. Following the collapse of A.T.&T. the following spring KLM recommenced flights between the two capitals using it's own aircraft.

> ## AIRCO PLEASURE FLIGHTS
>
> OWING to the large demand we have received from the public, we have arranged that short flights may be taken daily from Croydon Aerodrome as follows :
>
> For a short flight round Croydon, during which London may be seen in the distance the charge is - £1 1s. 0d. per passenger.
>
> For a longer flight, during which a magnificent view of London is obtained the charge is -   £2 5s. 0d. per passenger.
>
> Tickets may be obtained at Croydon Aerodrome, 27 Pall Mall, S.W.1., and all usual agencies.

Airco Advertisment for Pleasure Flights, Summer 1920

On 10th June Capt. Baylis was forced to land the new Napier Lion powered Airco 16, G-EARU, at the Marden emergency landing ground due to a faulty carburettor. The passengers continued their journey by road and following repairs by an A.T.&T. Engineer Baylis took off at 10 pm for Croydon with Mr Hall, the Airco engineer, and the owners of the landing ground, Mr.& Mrs. Day.

It was dusk, and Baylis soon found that he was unable to read his compass in the failing light, and with a ground mist forming he soon lost his bearings and attempted a landing in a field of wheat near Swanley. The aircraft nosed over and Mrs Day sustained serious back injuries. The Inspector of Accidents noted that even though Baylis had been flying long after nightfall the aircraft was not equipped with navigation lights, the compass light had been disconnected and that the luminous lettering on the compass had deteriorated, making it impossible to obtain a reading in the darkness. Surprisingly, the airworthiness requirements in force at the time did not include any requirements concerning the serviceability of compasses and ground engineers were not required to possess any knowledge of these instruments, which helps to explain why attempting to navigate with an unreliable compass was often the lot of the first airline pilots.

By July A.T.&T. had further reduced the single fare on the London - Paris service to only £10, just above the "break-even" point if every seat on a flight was sold. Together with the good weather of the summer months this resulted in an increase in passenger numbers. Airco had also attempted to generate extra revenue by ad-hoc charter operations and Pleasure Flights, but the deteriorating state of the company's finances was now beginning to affect aircraft serviceability, resulting in a large number of forced landings and cancelled flights. On 2nd July Bill was flying the afternoon service to Paris in the Napier Lion powered Airco 16, G-EASW, when the engine oil pressure failed over the Channel:

"Engine oil pressure failed mid-Channel, had a 'near squeak' and sticky business. Vol Planing (gliding) into Lympne Aerodrome where I landed O.K. - stopped night at Lympne, sent passengers by boat etc."

Ground staff worked through the night on the aircraft, but after two test flights next day there was no improvement in oil pressure and with the likely cause down to bearing failure Bill and the maintenance crew left the aircraft at Lympne and returned to Croydon by train. Following this incident A.T.&T.'s Traffic Manager at Croydon Donald Greig received the following letter:

Dear Sir,

With Mr. And Mrs. Cannon, I was one of the passengers on the aeroplane in charge of Mr. Lawford, which was forced to make a landing at Lympne en route to Paris this evening. In the face of a strong head-wind the oil pressure failed when we were half-way across the Channel.

Mr. Lawford acted admirably and from his elevation of about 7,000 feet, turned and made for Lympne and, although he was running on a dry motor, he made a beautiful landing. I cannot speak with too great praise of Mr. Lawford's generalship and his handling of every detail. Had he not acted so quickly or so efficiently or wisely, I cannot be sure that we might not have found ourselves in a bad situation.

As I have experienced Mr. Lawford's skill and judgement as an aviator, it would not be fair to him or to you , to let this occurrence pass without telling you how I commend you for having such a man in your service.

Mr. And Mrs. Cannon join me in what I have said in this letter.

Very truly yours,

Edwin de T. Bechtel, General Counsel for the American Express Company

Passengers prepare to embark on the Airco 16, G-EASW, at Croydon

The A.J. Jackson Collection at Brooklands Museum

On the evening of 20th July Bill made his last flight from Croydon to Le Bourget carrying four passengers in the Airco 16, G-EALM, with a very rough engine which was misfiring and overheating. The next morning he left LeBourget for Croydon with four passengers, but was forced to return to Le Bourget when the liquid cooled Rolls-Royce Eagle VIII engine again started to misfire badly and temperature of the coolant increased to 97 degrees centigrade. After repairs and a test flight the engine still had problems and it was decided to ferry the aircraft back to Croydon for repair work. Bill set off for Croydon but approaching Lympne he ran into low cloud and was forced to land on the coast at Lydd to wait for the weather to clear. After landing at Lympne to refuel he continued on to Croydon. On arrival he reported that the aircraft's engine was *"dreadful"*, and recommended a complete overhaul. This was Bill's last flight as a pilot. The rigours and stresses encountered during almost a year of flying in all weathers had slowly taken a toll on his health and he transferred to a ground job, spending the next two months managing the Airco and A.T.&T workshops, where he was responsible for the maintenance of about 25 aircraft.

At the end of the summer of 1920 a major management shake-up took place at A.T.&T. Sir Sefton Brancker resigned, and was replaced as Managing Director by Col. Frank Searle. Searle had previously been Manager of the London Omnibus Company, and during June 1919 he had been appointed as Managing Director of the Daimler Hire Co, part of the B.S.A. Group of Companies, which specialised in luxury car hire. Encouraged by George Holt-Thomas, the deHavilland Aircraft Co. was formed on 25th September 1920 by Airco's chief designer, Geoffrey deHavilland, and other former members of the Airco management team. Airco's jigs and tooling were purchased from B.S.A. Ltd. for a nominal sum, and the new company set up in business further along the Edgware road at Stag Lane to continuing production of the Airco 18, now known as the deHavilland 18. The subsidised French Airlines continued to undercut A.T.&T's fares and the fortunes of the Company were now very much in decline. Although the Civil Aviation Committee had recommended limited assistance for the struggling British Airlines during June, the Government had adopted a waiting policy in the hope that the airlines would pull through the crisis unassisted, but with the approach of winter and the prospect of further disruption of flights due to the weather, the future for A.T.&T. was bleak. Aware that the Company was facing a very uncertain future, Bill submitted his resignation on 22nd September 1920.[10] George Holt-Thomas was pessimistic:

"In answer to your letter which I have just received I am afraid that I cannot be of much use to you. I well remember the qualifications you possess, but of course there are not many positions worth taking in aviation at the present moment. If I hear of anything likely to be of use to you, I will certainly let you know."

The dire situation facing the British airline industry was also summed up in a letter that Bill received from Branker following his resignation:

"If I hear of anything in the aviation world likely to suit you I will certainly recommend you thoroughly. You did excellently with A.T.&T. and I am very sorry that you have left the Company. As you know, at present, there is very

---

[10] See Appendix 5, Documents, page 4

little real development going on in aviation, but next spring should see some movement and progress."

A.T.&T's continued operations during October and November 1920 achieving reasonable traffic figures, but the onset of winter weather and continuing absence of Government assistance together with the low level of fares charged to remain competitive with the subsidised French carriers eventually proved unsustainable. On 9th December a receiver was appointed and it was reported that the Company was insolvent. An optimistic Frank Searle stated that services would continue, but after struggling on for a further week the Company was forced to cease operations on the 17th December 1920 when the parent company, Airco, was put into liquidation by B.S.A. Ltd. The assets of A.T.&T. were later acquired by the Daimler Hire Company which began aircraft operation as the Daimler Airway Ltd. A disillusioned Sir Sefton Brancker commented that:

"Aircraft Transport and Travel has withered away through lack of financial support and assistance from the Government."

Bill Lawford Taxying Airco 9b, G-EAQN, at Croydon, 1920

Hillyer Collection, via Albert E. Smith and Croydon Airport Society

The majority of the Airco and A.T.&T. employees who had worked hard to keep the two struggling companies afloat did not remain unemployed for long. Three months later the government belatedly granted limited operational subsidies to A.T.&T's competitors, Handley Page Air Transport and the Instone Airline, and these companies were able to take on many of A.T.&T's redundant staff when operations recommenced on the London - Paris and other Continental routes on 19th March 1921. In April 1921 the Dutch airline K.L.M. recommenced operations with it's own aircraft following a winter break, and employed many British pilots until sufficient Dutch nationals could be trained. Albert Plesman, the founder of KLM, had been so impressed with the efficient way that Capt. Henry Spry-Leverton had looked after the comfort of A.T.&T. passengers by providing the heavy fur lined flying clothing required for passengers travelling in the open cockpits of the Airco 9's, that he appointed him as KLM's Station Manager at Croydon. Later, more A.T.&T. staff were taken on by the Daimler Airway which began operations with Airco 18's in August 1921 under A.T.&T's former Managing Director, Frank Searle.

A Change of Course

Following his resignation from Aircraft Transport and Travel Ltd. Bill found that he was unable to settle down to a career away from aviation. In a depressed post war economy employment was difficult to find, and after a couple of years Bill decided to return to a career in aviation. He still had many old friends and colleagues in the industry, and during May 1923 the following item entitled *"An Old Timer Coming Back"* appeared in the aviation weekly, "Flight":

"Quite by accident we ran up against one of the old-timers the other day in the street. After the usual exclamations, questions and answers it transpired that the aforesaid old-timer, Bill Lawford, who apart from being one of the pre-war Hendon pilots, was one of the heroic band of pilots who demonstrated to a wondering world what could be done in the way of air transport when Mr. Holt-Thomas started the A.T.and T .in 1919, thought that he could be happy away from aviation, and is now beginning to find that he can't. After doing exceedingly good work for the A.T. and T, Lawford retired from actual flying and turned his attentions to more prosaic pursuits, chiefly out of consideration for his old mother. He was never quite happy, however, in work that did not have about it the smell of petrol and oil, and has now decided that there is nothing for it but to return to aviation. Lawford needs no introduction to the aircraft industry, and the mere mention of him being willing to return "to the fold" should be sufficient. He will undertake piloting if necessary, although he would, we think, prefer some ground job in the experimental department. It might be mentioned that apart from being a good pilot Lawford is a wizard with machines and engines, and in the old days when he was at Farnborough, it used to be said if he could not tune up a machine then certainly nobody else could and the ' bus had better be burnt. If any firm wants a really good man with ten years experience and will write to the Editor of Flight, letters will be forwarded promptly."

"Flight's" recommendation did not go unnoticed at the Air Ministry. Bill's old boss at A.T.& T, Sir Sefton Brancker, had recently been appointed as Director General of Civil Aviation, and he arranged for Bill to take up a position as a Civil Aviation Traffic Officer in the Control Tower at Croydon Airport, under the Airport's Chief Civil Aviation Traffic Officer, Capt. Stanley Baker.

The urgent need for some form of control for air traffic had been underlined in April 1921, when a DH18 of the Daimler Airway flying from Croydon to Le Bourget collided with a Farman Goliath belonging to Grands Express Aeriens near Grandvilliers in northern France. This was the first mid-air collision between aircraft operating on the London – Paris route, and all the occupants of

The Direction Finding Cabin at Croydon Airport, c.1922

This was the world's first dedicated Airport Conrol Tower, popularily known as "The Cucumber Frame", following the construction of the glass roofed cabin above the original hut

Croydon Airport Society

both aircraft lost their lives. As was customary on the route, the pilots had been following the road between Beauvais and Abbeville, flying at approximately 400 feet in poor visibility on reciprocal tracks. Although radio communications equipment had been in use at both Croydon and Le Bourget Airports for some time there was no requirement for aircraft to carry radio equipment and collision avoidance was dependant upon each pilot maintaining a good lookout for other aircraft. In the misty conditions neither pilot saw the other aircraft in time to avoid a collision. The official report into this accident found that the poor forward view from the cockpit of the DH18 and the failure of both pilots to remain at least 100 yards to the right of the surface feature that they were following, as required by the regulations then in force, had contributed to the accident. This accident resulted in the implementation of defined routes to be followed by commercial aircraft operating between Croydon and Le Bourget. Later, further defined routes between Croydon and other major European capitals were introduced, but most pilots continued to ignore the "keep to the right" rule. Air traffic had grown rapidly following the introduction of government subsidies for the beleaguered British airlines, and it was essential to reassure the travelling public that a system of safe air traffic control was in operation to prevent further mid-air collisions and ensure safe en-route separation of aircraft.

    Bill joined the small team of Air Ministry Civil Aviation Traffic Officers working in the Direction Finding Cabin at Croydon Aerodrome, including Capt. J.P. Morkham, and an old colleague from A.T.&T, H.W. Chattaway, who had recently retired from flying with the Instone Airline, and "Jimmy" Jeffs, later appointed as Chief Aerodrome Officer at Croydon and holder of Air Traffic Control Officer's Licence No.1 when the formal licensing of air traffic controllers was introduced some twenty years later.

The first Air Traffic Control unit in the world was housed in a small wooden hut about 8 feet square mounted on a steel support frame, about 12 feet above ground level, known as the "Direction Finding Cabin". Reached by means of a ladder it was staffed by a duty traffic officer assisted by a radio operator who could communicate by voice with aircraft as far away as Paris or Amsterdam using Radio Telephony (R/T), or by Wireless Telephony (W/T) in morse code. Radio Direction Finding equipment at Croydon and two outstations situated at Pulham, Norfolk and Lympne in Kent, which could obtain bearings from the radio transmissions of aircraft en-route were introduced during 1922, and by using a system of triangulation it was often possible to fix an aircraft's position within a minute of receiving a request by radio. The system was put to the test on the morning of the 16th April 1925 when gale force winds caused the Government Airship R.33 to break away from it's mooring mast at Pulham, under the command of Flight Lieut. R.S. Booth with an anchor crew of 20 men on board. For the next 28 hours the traffic staff at Croydon maintained radio contact with badly damaged airship, logging it's position as it drifted helplessly downwind over the North Sea towards the Dutch coast, passing information on the position of the stricken airship to their colleagues on the Continent in case their assistance was needed. Bill was one of the team on duty at Croydon that night and he decribed the incident:

"For more than 24 hours we at Croydon maintained a feverish watch with the atmosphere crammed full of vital wireless messages from the Airship and foreign wireless stations. Slowly the great Airship drifted away to the coast of Holland, shadowed by the gunboat, "Godetia", and we had to sit and wait for what we considered would be the inevitable S.O.S. We were informed by radio from Paris, Cologne, Amsterdam, Brussels and many other foreign Airports that they were all standing by with the Military and Landing Parties, in case the 'lame duck' could make any one of these Airports. However it proved that owing to the consummate skill of the Captain and crew they were able to keep the Airship's nose in to wind, whilst they drifted to leeward all through that terribly stormy night. As dawn broke we received the first ray of hope - a wireless message from the distressed craft - "Holding weigh over the Dutch coast" - and a little later - "Making three knots" - and as the morning wore on - "Making good five, six and so on knots" - and then - "Passing the English coast" - at which enthusiasm broke the bounds of discipline, and the Direction Finding Cabin echoed with resounding cheers. Finally, when news came that she had been successfully landed, our watch finished, we struggled white-faced wearily

The badly damaged R.33 is safely secured at Pulham following the breakaway

off to bed with feelings of elation that we had 'done our bit' to help in averting a catastrophe."

Passenger traffic at Croydon increased only slowly during the early 1920's, but in 1924 the Airport began a period of rapid growth. Following the near collapse of the British air transport industry in the spring of 1921 a reluctant government had provided temporary subsidies to the two surviving British international airlines, Handley Page Air Transport and the Instone Airline. Early in 1922 these two companies were joined on the London - Paris route by the Daimler Airway, created out of the ashes of A.T.&T. by former Managing Director, Col. Frank Searle. In 1923, the Government appointed a Committee under Sir Herbert Hambling, Chairman of Barclays Bank, to determine how best to support cross-channel air services in the future. By early 1924, following the recommendations of this Committee, these three companies and the British Marine Air Navigation Co. were brought together to form a new, subsidised, national air transport company, Imperial Airways Ltd, with Frank Searle appointed as Managing Director. Efficient control of the growing volume of air traffic using the air routes between the Continent and Imperial Airway's base at Croydon was now essential if a largely sceptical public was to be convinced that air travel was safe.

The limitations of Croydon aerodrome and its facilities, which had received little improvement since the R.A.F. had moved out, were now evident.

Eight lives had been lost on Christmas Eve 1924 when an Imperial Airways DH 34 attempting to take off to the south west failed to get airborne on the uphill gradient, and this crash was one of the factors which led to a plan for a major redevelopment of the Airport. The existing airport buildings clustered along Plough Lane were to be replaced by a new purpose built terminal building with an adjacent hotel to be built along the eastern boundary of the Airport and serviced by a new road, the Purley Way, linking Waddon and Purley. Demolition of the Plough Lane complex allowed the adjacent Beddington aerodrome site to be incorporated into the existing Airport, greatly extending the area available for landing and take off and providing a greater margin of safety in difficult weather conditions.

Bill and his colleagues worked closely on issues concerning safety with the pilots using Croydon, and many problems were discussed when the pilots and airport personnel gathered for a few drinks after work in the bar of the old Airport Hotel operated by Trust Houses Ltd, and situated in the former RAF Officer's Mess at Plough Lane. Bill found himself amongst many old friends and colleagues, and with the camaraderie which existed within the small aviation community at Croydon he was usually invited to the cockpit during his off duty trips to the Continent, often taking the controls of the aircraft to indulge in some unofficial piloting.

Early in 1926 he flew as a passenger on a series of flights around the south of England with Franklyn Barnard and Col. Freddy Minchin in the Bristol Bloodhound, G-EBGG, which had been fitted with a Bristol Jupiter engine as part of that engine's flight test programme. He also made trips to Paris, Brussels and Cologne in the Handley Page W.8's of Imperial Airways and during March 1927 he had the chance to take the controls of one of the new Armstrong Whitworth "Argosy" airliners of Imperial Airways during a flight test over the Croydon area with Captain Jimmy Youell.

During May 1927 he was part of a team including the D.C.A., Sir Sefton Brancker, representatives from the Marconi Company and the R.AeE. Farnborough, which carried out a two and a half hour survey flight at night to check the radio and night lighting facilities on the British section of the London - Paris airway. The flight was made in the Air Ministry operated Vickers Vanguard, G-EBCP, piloted by Capt. Oddie, routeing from Croydon to Maidstone and along the North Kent coast to South Foreland from where the Calais light was clearly visible. The St.Inglevert light was described as "dim", but the revolving beacon at Cap Gris Nez was described as "splendid". Returning via Eastbourne and Tonbridge, the Penshurst light was recorded as "flashing, very weak", Tatsfield "flashing White-Red-White, very good indeed" and the Croydon revolving floodlight and neon arc lights as "splendid", a contemporary assessment of the efficiency of early night navigation beacons on the northern section of the Croydon-Paris route.

There was no formal system of licensing for the Air Ministry Control Officers at Croydon, but all were required to hold or have held a "B" (Commercial) Pilot's Licence, and additionally, from 1927, they were also required to obtain an Aircraft Navigator's Licence. After sitting the relevant examinations Bill was granted Aircraft Navigator's Licence No.29, 2nd Class, on 25th October 1927.

On 30th January 1928 the newly completed Terminal Buildings on Purley Way were opened for business, but it was not until the 25th April, just ahead of the official opening by Lady Maude Hoare on 2nd May, that Bill and his colleagues transferred to the new Control Tower which dominated the airside frontage of the new complex. Major Leslie F. Richard had replaced Capt. Stanley Baker as C.A.T.O. in charge at Croydon early in 1926, and Bill and his colleagues in the Control Tower were now officially known as "Aerodrome Officers," and responsible for the operation of the Airport on a day to day basis under "Jimmy" Jeffs, who had been appointed as Chief Aerodrome Officer. The system of direction finding equipment used in the new Control Tower to fix an aircraft's position in flight was similar to that used in the first Control Cabin at the Plough Lane site. Aircraft positions fixed by D/F bearings were plotted by pinning a small flag carrying the aircraft's identification on a special map of the airspace between London and Paris. This was later replaced by a map with metal backing and magnetic markers to identify each aircraft's position. Bill described the new Control Tower and the methods used to provide navigational assistance and guidance for air traffic :

"Above the main Airport Administration Building there is a large glass-enclosed Room about 30 feet square, some fifty to sixty feet high, surmounted by a tall wireless mast. This room is divided into two compartments - the Navigating Room and the Wireless Room. The former, occupied by the Duty Officer, is equipped with the most modern flying maps and charts, Air Navigating Instruments, and a series of switches which control all the apparatus for instantly lighting up the Aerodrome and bringing into operation Aerial Beacons, flood lights, obstruction lights, landing lights etc.

Direct telephones provide communication to the Meteorological and other technical departments and various operating Companies, the whole idea being to centralise all intelligence in, and disseminate it from the Control Tower, which has been referred to as the "Brain of the Airways".

The second compartment - glass screened and sound proof against engine noise - is the Wireless Room in which are two wireless experts constantly tuning in to the various aircraft in flight. The Duty Officer has a loudspeaker in his Navigating Room, so that he too can listen to the various machines, and tell the wireless operators to give the necessary instructions or information to the aeroplanes concerned, for he has in front of him a large map about six feet square of all the flying routes, and upon this map by means of small flags he pinpoints or dots the position of all aircraft actually in the air. This he is able to do by virtue of the fact that he is an old pilot and air navigator who is thoroughly conversant with all the country over which civil aeroplanes fly, and of which ineffaceable mental picture. Thus, knowing the cruising speed of each type of machine, and having access to all the latest meteorological information, he can calculate by means of his instruments the approximate position of any machine at any time, and it is essential that this be done every few minutes - for there may be about ten machines leaving England for France, Belgium, Holland and Germany, and a similar number coming the opposite way all converging over the Channel at the same time, and it is the Control Officers duty to refer to his map and warn machines of others approaching or near them and to issue instructions to the machines concerned to take specified aerial corridors, and fly at stipulated heights, so that fro instance those approaching the French coast will be taking one route at a certain height, and those approaching the English coast another route at another height. This avoids any possibility of collision or confusion. The Control officer then wirelesses by Radio-telephony all the latest weather reports, so that the aerial liners may be prevented from running into danger owing to foul weather, Sometimes they instructed to land at intermediate aerodromes, rather than venture onwards.

  It may come as a surprise to some travellers by air to learn that although a machine may be temporarily off it's course and not know it's exact whereabouts owing to clouds or fog, that we at Croydon operating in conjunction with other ground stations, can within one and a half minutes locate it's precise position by means of Radio-Goniometric direction-finding apparatus, and the pilot on receiving this by wireless refers to his map and compares it with the position he thought he might be at, judging from the time that he has been flying and the compass course taken, and after making a rapid calculation alters course accordingly. Fifteen minutes later he may ask for another position and if this corresponds approximately with the place he expects to be at, he knows he is on the right course, if not he again asks a few minutes later for another wireless position, and so the process continues, it being seen that each time the error gets less and less until he is near his destination. An easy way for a pilot who is above the clouds or in fog to reach his aerodrome is to ask for a course to fly on, in which case one D/F station alone takes a bearing on the machine and passes the reciprocal bearing, e.g. "Your course to Croydon is 310 degrees true," the pilot then makes allowance for compass variation and deviation and steers the resultant course. On the same principle as with D/F positions, by asking for courses at intervals he is bound to correct his error and arrive near hid destination. Within three or four miles of the Aerodrome, however, it is difficult to get an exact position or bearing, and we can only tell the pilot the he is North, South, East or West and so on of the aerodrome, but by this time he has probably seen our Neon flashing beacon light and revolving floodlight and ground flares, but if not, on hearing engines, we tell hime to look

Bill Lawford with slide-rule and an early map of the London - Paris air route. in the Croydon Control Tower, 1928. The small flags were pinned to this map to show the estimated position of each aircraft

E.H. Lawford Archive

out for a series of pyrotechnics in the shape of Magnesium Flares and Star Shells which are projected to about 1000 feet for his guidance. Finally, when he has located the Aerodrome, the floodlight is lowered so that it spreads a fan shaped beam of diffused light right across the Aerodrome, making it almost like day, and the machine lands down this light and along the flares which are arranged in the shape of a 'T' to indicate the direction of the wind into which the machine, for safety, must always land. Now let us imagine are on watch with the Duty Officer in the Control Tower. Let us say that the night flying machines which left Paris at 12.30 arrived OK at 3 am, and the Duty Officer has had his "forty winks" and is "up again with the Lark". It is very early morning. On the lofty gallery surrounding the Control Tower the look-out man is posted to watch the movements of aircraft on the Aerodrome, whilst constantly scanning the horizon for incoming aeroplanes. Immediately below is a large paved area called the apron or tarmac, to which all incoming aircraft, having landed, taxi to "disemplane" passengers and goods and upon which all outgoing aircraft line up in rotation to "emplane" voyagers and freight. Customs, Immigration and C.I.D. Officials are all present, the formalities being exactly the same as one would expect at a sea port except that they are carried out and got through very much more comfortably and swiftly. Several machines of various nationalities, British, French, Belgian, German, Dutch and sometimes Swedish and Italian, are now ready with their engines "ticking over", they have all been inspected and passed airworthy by the Ground Engineers and are ready to depart according to our Air Timetable.

All at once the look out hails the Duty Officer with "Imperial ready to depart - all clear." The Duty Officer, having satisfied himself that it is all clear replies "Let her go." A disc bearing the initials of the company to whom the aircraft belongs is displayed, and she taxies out on to the Aerodrome and takes up position in to wind. The look-out now calls "Imperial ready to take-off.....all clear, and gives his approval. A searchlight from the Control Tower is then focussed upon the plane and away she goes. One after another aircraft depart in this manner at short intervals until the atmosphere reverberates with the droning roar of aero engines, and each is watched by vigilant eyes and ears attuned to detect any possible fault which would be immediately communicated to the pilot by wireless. The Route Map in the Control Tower mentioned earlier now fairly bristles with little flags - signifying the markings and positions of the various aircraft. In a short while a cosmopolitan babel of sound issues from the loudspeaker and our wireless friends have a very hectic time. This is the sort of thing - "Allo Croirdon, Allo Croirdon - Goliath Ah Bey vous appelle, nous faisons route pour Le Bourget, et nous passons Bee-gin-ill, voulez vous me donnez le temps de Lympne, s'il vous plait. Je vous accoute." The deep voices of Dutch and German pilots are heard asking for weather conditions etc., and so it goes on all day.

Of the twenty or more machines now flying probably a dozen may be about to cross the Channel, say fro example six outgoing and six incoming, and we hear this perhaps - "Hallo Croydon, Hallo Croydon, Imperial G-AACH calling, leaving Boulogne for Littlestone at 1000 feet, latest Lympne weather report please" - and then - "Allo Croirdon, Allo Croirdon, Air Union Ah Bey vous appelle, nous prennons le Mer a Folk-es-stone pour Boulogne - je vous accoute." Both these machines are replied to, when a facetious confrere in the Tower remarks "Nous prennons le Mer - indeed, what, are they pinching the blooming Channel?"

Obviously a very close watch is kept on all machines whilst they are over the Channel or "ditch" and the Meteorological Officers keep in close liaison with us giving immediate information as to any change or deterioration in cloud height or visibility.

As has already been explained, if necessary we call up all machines in the Channel vicinity, give them the latest weather reports, inform them of aircraft near or approaching them, and instruct them to fly at different heights. The radio-goniometer direction-finding apparatus is kept very active over this area.

After an hour or so the aircraft have all safely crossed and we have a breather, the next spasm being when several air liners of different nationalities are all trying to get into the Air Port of Croydon about the same time in foggy weather.

The Duty Officer has to act quickly and firmly, so, keeping his head (if not his temper) he instructs some machines to stand off while he signals one at time to land, this being sometimes accompanied by a pyrotechnical display of star shells and "Flaming Onions" of Magnesium, which are projected up to a height of about 1,000 feet.

When "all clear" messages have been received from all the other Aerodromes, and every aircraft has been definitely accounted for - then, and only then, may we close down for an hour or so until the night flying starts. However, one Duty Officer is always available at the Aerodrome in case of emergency.

As "Old Wallahs" the Duty Officers, after long association, regard both British and foreign pilots as their brothers, and a wonderful camaraderie exists between us all; we constantly discuss all difficulties with a view to further efficiency and progress, and if we feel we have been helpful to the Pilots we are satisfied."

1929 was a busy year for Bill. The new Terminal Buildings and the mysteries of the Control Tower at Croydon had created widespread public interest and he was asked to give a radio talk on the new facilities by the B.B.C. which was broadcast during March. There were only four qualified Aerodrome Officers working at Croydon during 1929, a situation which resulted in long periods of duty and was aggravated further when H.W. Chattaway and Capt. John Morkham absented themselves for extended periods of sick leave, putting considerable extra demands on Bill and Jimmy Jeffs to cover their periods of absence. To ease this situation the highly experienced navigator, Squadron Leader E.L. Jackson, was employed by the Air Ministry for the summer months on a temporary contract at Croydon.

August 25th 1929 marked the tenth anniversary of regular air services and Bill reflected on the progress made since the first London - Paris service:

"The development that has taken place in Commercial Aviation during the past ten years can truly be described as amazing when one compares the modern multi-engine twenty seat airliners with the old converted war planes with which a start was made on August 25th 1919 at Hounslow aerodrome. In those dear old Airco days we had no wireless and outward traffic consisted of one or two machines daily, each carrying two or three passengers who had to be squeezed into tiny seats or sandwiched in amongst parcels and baggage.

Foreign weather reports were conspicuous by their absence and if any were received at all they were generally unintelligible. Here one cannot help repeating the hackneyed joke about a certain report received which read "Bolsons in the Channel and Squaggy", which called forth the remark that whatever these Bolsons might be it was about time that the minesweepers had cleared them all away! With this scanty information and words of encouragement such as "Stick it," the pilot would climb into the open cockpit and disappear into the blue.

"Bill" Lawford pictured at Croydon in 1929 with a group of his contemporaries all of whom had flown on the early cross Channel air services ten years before. From left to right Freddie Dismore, Walter Rogers, "Scruffy" Robinson, "Bill" Lawford, Herbert Perry and Gordon Olley.

Croydon Airport Society

In spite of the discomforts they put up a wonderful record for regularity in getting through to their destinations. It was sheer determination and loyalty to their Company, coupled with long war experience, that enabled them to fly in the worst of weather without any navigational aid whatsoever. Yes, they were wonderful days.

Today, as the outcome of years of patient research and practical trial, everything has been reduced to a scientific system - Safety First, Law, Order and Method. Our up-to-date multi-engined, twenty seat luxurious airliners, besides being equipped with numerous ingenious navigation instruments, are all provided with wireless, by means of which pilots keep in constant *communications with several ground stations spread over England and the Continent."*

Bill had many opportunities to make flights abroad with the airlines using Croydon. At the end of October 1929 Imperial Airways was forced to suspend operations on the Genoa - Athens sector of the air route to India which had only opened that spring. The entire Mediterranean flying boat fleet of three Short Calcutta's had been put out of action with the loss of G-AADN off Spezia, and serious hull damage which been sustained by the remaining two Short Calcutta's G-EBVG and 'VU. The problem was exacerbated on the 31st October when the Italian government refused the use of their ports to British flying boats as Imperial Airways had refused to pool the revenues earned on the Genoa - Alexandria section of the route with the Italian operator. This prompted a search for an alternative route through the Balkans to Athens, from where the service to India could continue from the Greek flying boat base at Phaeleron Bay on to Cairo, using a Supermarine Southampton flying boat hastily borrowed from the Air Ministry.

A flight to survey the proposed new Balkan air route departed from Croydon on the 2nd November 1929, under the command of Capt. L.A. Walters flying Armstrong Whitworth Argosy G-EBLF, with the Director of Civil Aviation, Sir W. Sefton Brancker, also on board. One week later A.W. Argosy, G-EBOZ, departed from Croydon on a second flight to survey the route, flown by one of Imperial Airways most experienced pilots, Capt. Walter Rogers, accompanied by two Imperial Airways engineers, Mr. Parker and Mr. Appelby. Bill had known Walter Rogers since the early days of the London - Paris service when Rogers had flown on the route for Handley-Page Air Transport, was also aboard and he wrote an account of this flight. It was the last flight to be operated by Imperial Airways on the Balkan route that winter as both Captains Walters and Rogers made adverse reports about the safety of the route on their return, emphasising the risk of attempting to operate a regular service through the mountainous Balkan terrain during the winter months, resulting in a decision to suspend flights on the route until the following spring. Bill's account of the flight to Athens with Rogers aboard G-EBOZ gives an insight in to the vagaries of air travel during the late 1920's:

"Departed Croydon at 0830 on Saturday 9th November with Rogers, Parker and Appelby in G-EBOZ for Cologne lovely trip at 4000' with following wind, landed at 1120. Departed Cologne at 1225 for Nurnberg - very sticky misty trip at 2000' across Taunus Mountains, had to follow the Rhine via Wiesbaden and Frankfurt due to mist on mountain tops. Arrived Nurnberg at 1450, where we met Travers with G-EBMR. Stayed at the Hotel Deutcherhof.

<u>Sunday 10th</u>

"Left Nurmberg for Vienna at 1155, very sticky weather at first, then better - followed the Danube - saw "Valhalla" at Regensberg also Austrian Tyrol - marvellous scenery - passed through the "Irongates" near Passau. Frightfully bumpy getting in to Vienna and all across the Jura Mountains and Austrian Alps. Landed at 1525 and overnighted at the Hotel Tegetthof."

A twenty passenger Armstrong Whitworth Argosy Airliner of Imperial Airways

via Croydon Airport Society

<u>Monday 11th</u>

"Vienna to Budapest at 0940, a frightfully sticky trip all along the Danube mountain passes. We passed Argosy G-EBLF returning home with Walters and the D.C.A. (Sir Sefton Brancker) at 1010 between Pressburg and Komorn, and landed Budapest at 1145.

1510 Budapest to Belgrade, across the Hungarian Plains, lovely weather latter half of the flight, arriving 1550. Stopped at Zeemoon Hotel and went to Cabaret. I never saw such a mixture of Slavs, gypsies and brigands - militarism and drilling everywhere."

Tuesday 12th

"Tried to get away for Uskub at 1113, but mist right down to river surface. We nearly hit a half completed bridge, so returned to Zeemoon and watched soldiers drilling and officers pulling them about disgracefully. We eventually got away at 1500, terribly rough flight over mountain passes at between 4000' and 7000'. No chances of landing anywhere due to huge glaciers etc., and impossible to fly under 5000', arrived at Uskub at 1500. Uskub (Skopje) used to be part of Turkey. Never saw such a mixture, Croats, Serbs, Bulgars, Turks, Gypsies, Brigands and all sorts of cut-throats. We stayed at the Hotel Bristol, and had a fine time at the Cabaret with Rogers and O'Shea the English Consul.

Bill, Walter Rogers and colleagues relaxing at the Parthenon, Athens, November 1929

E.H. Lawford Archive

<u>Wednesday 13th</u>

"0943 Uskub to Selonica, via Monastir and Florino, enormous snow-clad mountains up to 10,000 feet - not a hope of landing anywhere. Arrived Salonika at 1150. Departed at 1425 for Athens, marvellous scenery over Mountains and Aegean Archipeligo, passing Mounts Olympus and Ossa visibility about 150 miles. Quite a reception for us at Tatoi Aerodrome where we arrived at 1650."

Bill and Rogers spent the next two days sightseeing in Athens and visited the flying boat base at Phaleron Bay before departing for the return trip to Croydon. They were accompanied as far as Salonica by Mr.Theodorides, a Greek Government Minister, and Mr. Harvey, a British Government Minister, and his wife.

"Left Athens for Salonica at 1430, marvellous visibility over Archipeligo, we saw the Dardanelles in the distance. Terrific bumps over Mounts Velos, Ossa and Olympus (Vardar Wind). We rose from 6000 to 8000 feet and then parachuted down from 8000 to 5000 feet and almost went out of control - both Rogers and myself hanging on to the controls endeavoring to keep the aircraft level. We had to alter course out to sea, and finally got out of the sort of whirlwind at 3000 feet - most alarming: Greek Officers told us at Salonica that we had had a very near squeak, as many machines had been wrecked over that area. Had a long yarn with the British and Greek Ministers that evening, and washed in the Aegean Sea as is the Custom."

They continued in good weather next day along the Vardar Valley to Uskub, and thence to Belgrade. From Belgrade to Budapest weather conditions deteriorated again:

"Raining and very low cloud, improving towards Budapest, arrived at 1550. Had a long pow-wow with Dr. Yahl of Ungarish Airlines over tea at the Ritz, and a quick look around the city in his car. To Parisienne Palace for Dinner, lovely city. Also met Travers again on the Handley-Page W 10, G-EBMR."

The engineers, Parker and Appelby, spent the evenings checking over the Argosy to ensure that the aircraft was serviceable for the following day's flying, and usually missed the social life enjoyed by the rest of the crew on the night stops. At Budapest Mr. Barnard joined the flight. He had arrived by rail from Croydon carrying the next consignment of Air Mail for India, but had now been instructed to return to Croydon in the Argosy following a decision to abandon the Athens service following the adverse report on the route made by Capt.

Walters on his return to Croydon. The Argosy departed from Budapest for the next leg to Vienna which took just under two hours flying time:

" *Very bad weather to start, improving towards Vienna, clouds on the mountains again, had to follow the river very closely. "Come up to the cockpit and give the mechanic a spell Bill," the skipper invited me at one stage. So up front I went. Oil consumption on the centre engine was always high on the Argosy, so I had a drum of oil on my side which I regularly pumped in to the engine which regularly threw it back on to the windscreen, so when I wasn't pumping I was wiping. Then we started through the mountain valleys - the old Argosy wasn't capable of going 'over the top'. "The routes all been set out for us," says little Rogers. "Its all in the flippin' book, so there can't be anythin' to worry about, can there?" Every now and again the valley would turn - and we'd turn with it. The bends got sharper and sharper until there was one which no Argosy could ever get round. "This must be where we climb over a flippin' saddle," says Mon Capitaine. We're no sooner over it than we're in the daddy of all updrafts, hurtling towards the sky. "Git yer feet in Bill, an' 'elp me 'old th' perishers nose down!" Yelled Rodge - and he meant it. All the time she's shuddering and trying to stall. Next instant we're dropping faster than when we came up. I couldn't believe there was such turbulence, but we eventually got through. "Lovely, tell yer Mum!" commented Rodge.[11] "*

After overnighting in Vienna they took off for Nurnberg arriving at 11:45 am after another flight through low cloud and mist, continuing on to Brussels at 5000 feet, above the cloudbase, navigating by dead reckoning as far as Frankfurt, and then via Aachen and Liege to Brussels, where they landed at 16:40 pm. They decided to spend the night at Brussels following a bad weather report from Croydon, and continued the flight next day, arriving home on the morning of the 20th November, only one day behind schedule. Bill summarised the trip:

"And so ended a most enjoyable and eventful flight across Europe, passing through eleven countries. The most interesting and dangerous part was Monastir to Florino at 8000 feet and the Greek Valley to Salonica. Going, the weather was very bad indeed and we had to dodge mountain sides and tops in the valleys. Returning we had terrific bumps over Mount Olympus and Ossa which nearly put us out of control."

---

[11] With acknowledgements to Ian Driscoll's book "Flightpath South Pacific", published by Whitcombe and Tombs.

Following the unsuccessful attempts to find a new air route through the to Balkans to Greece, Imperial Airways re-routed the Indian Air Mail by train from Paris to Athens where it connected with their flying boat service to Egypt, an arrangement which also turned out to be much cheaper!

And so ended a decade which had started with Bill flying as one of the small group of pioneer British airline pilots, and during which he had made a transition to a new career, joining the small group of Air Ministry personnel engaged in pioneering the early systems evolving to prevent mid-air collisions and assist air navigation which would later develop into a formal system of Air Traffic Control.

The Golden Era at Croydon

British air transport had grown rapidly during the 1920's, dominated by Imperial Airways, the government backed "Chosen Instrument", established in 1924 largely due to the foresight and effort of Sir Sefton Branker, now Director of Civil Aviation (D.C.A.) at the Air Ministry. Larger and more efficient aircraft had brought about some reduction in fare levels, which together with the introduction of new air routes serving Europe and the Empire and increasing activity by foreign airlines resulted in a steady growth of air traffic at Croydon. The Airport, it's newly built Terminal Buildings and the adjacent the Aerodrome Hotel, was now the focal point of what is often remembered as the "Golden Era" of British air transport. There was now a definite air of optimism for the future of the airline industry. The pilots and Control Tower staff frequented a special "Pilot's Room" at the Aerodrome Hotel, which was operated along the lines of a select private club. The oak panelled walls of the Pilot's Room were adorned with caricatures of Airport personalities drawn by artist Charles Dickson, and Bill's caricature[12] was described thus:

"Some say that the one of Bill Lawford is the best. He is now an officer in the Control Tower, and every morning he arrives at the aerodrome in the most amazing Austin Seven that ever crawled out of it's shell. It is embellished with every gadget conceived of man. It's proud owner has an amazing vocabulary all his own. His fantastic gadgets he calls "Doo-hickies," and there is something of a celebration at Croydon when yet another doo-hickey is added to the long suffering Austin. Then again, Mr. Bill Lawford never drives, motors, journeys, moves or progresses in this car of his. He "teedles." He is always "teedling" somewhere. All of which explains the caricature of the diminutive car that looks as though it were caught in a spider's web, and the cheery "teedle, teedle!" issuing from the exhaust."

During February 1930 Bill was transferred on a temporarily posting to Lympne Airport, Kent, to relieve the resident C.A.T.O, Commander Deacon. Lympne still acted as an important diversion aerodrome for Croydon when Imperial Airway's preferred alternate aerodrome at Heston was closed by bad weather. The quiet routine at Lympne was interrupted on 10th February when Bill received an urgent summons to the emergency landing ground at Marden, between Ashford and Tonbridge, to carry out an initial investigation into the crash of an Air Union Farman Goliath, F-FHMY. The Goliath had been attempting to make an emergency landing at Marden but burst into flames on

---

[12] See Appendix 5, page 9

touchdown, tragically killing a newly married couple returning to Croydon after their honeymoon in Paris.

During his time at Lympne Bill had the opportunity to fly a deHavilland Cirrus Moth for the first time before returning to Croydon. The aircraft belonged to the Cinque Ports Flying Club, and in spite of the gusty weather he was very impressed with the aircraft's ease of handling. The advent of a new generation of affordable light aircraft had resulted in the rapid growth of private flying and by the autumn Bill had flown in many new types including a Desoutter Monoplane, a Blackburn Bluebird and the new deHavilland "Puss Moth". As an Official Observer for the Royal Aero Club Bill was often called on to pass out pilots for their "A" Licence at Penshurst, Addington, Gatwick and Croydon aerodromes, passing a young Geoffrey Last for his "A" Licence in November 1932. Almost 27 years later, on the evening of 30th September 1959, Capt. Geoffrey Last would command the final scheduled service to depart from Croydon before the Airport's closure.

During April 1930 Bill flew to Basle with Imperial Airways in the Handley Page W.10, "City of Pretoria", spending some time at the aircraft's controls as usual, and later in the month he had the opportunity to fly the new Avro 619 tri-motor with Capt. O.P. Jones, making three landings at Croydon.

At the end of April the seasonal traffic at Croydon had started to build up, and the rapidly increasing number of private aircraft flying over the Channel to the continent were now causing problems for the Control Tower staff. Bill was very concerned, stating:

"The Control Tower staff have a pretty busy time and are now on what practically amounts to a continuous 24 hour watch. Owing to the selfish neglect on the part of many private owners to conform to regulations by circling the French coastal stations, and reporting their arrival at their destinations, the Control Tower, Duty Officer and wireless staff were put to the greatest trouble and confusion. When will some of these private owners realise that in disregarding these regulations which have been carefully thought out and framed for their own especial safety, they are endangering their professional brother pilots, who on large commercial machines with, perhaps, twenty passengers may be endeavouring to send wireless messages on account of real trouble, only to find themselves jammed out by wireless stations making all sorts of unnecessary enquiries in respect of a supposedly missing light plane which has not circled their station"

On 5th May Bill witnessed Amy Johnson's departure from Croydon on her successful attempt to complete the first solo flight by a woman pilot to Australia:

"Plucky Miss Amy Johnson departed on her long lone flight to Australia. It looked as though her machine was not going to "unstick" at first,

but she showed her sound judgement on shutting off and taxiing back to take the full run of the aerodrome, and at the second attempt made an excellent take-off."

Before the introduction of radio approach aids the Control Tower staff had become familiar with the many different techniques used by individual pilots to locate the Airport in bad weather, some of which caused them anxious moments. Bill described an approach and landing made by a Sabena aircraft in particularly difficult conditions caused by shallow fog:

"M. Cocquyt of Sabena ran into thick fog which came up suddenly at Croydon, Kenley and Biggin Hill, and although he could see the lights of these three aerodromes from above, it was impossible to distinguish anything near the ground.

After making several unsuccessful attempts between salvo's of star shells he finally adopted a clever piece of strategy - flying very low near the south-east corner of the aerodrome, where he knew that there were no buildings or obstructions, he crossed Purley Way at right angles, and taking a line on the Neon "Tee" dropped in below the Neon Beacon and gradually flattened out, knowing he had the best part of a mile of clear ground in front of him.

His landing was perfect, but so thick was the fog, that he had to await the arrival of the aerodrome tender to show him the way to taxy to the Tarmac. A wonderful effort of piloting, but, oh! the suspense to the onlookers!

Fifteen Prime Ministers from the Dominions made an official visit to Croydon during October 1930, and Bill was nominated as a guide to explain the everyday running of the Airport to the visitors. The Prime Ministers were taken on a special sightseeing flight over London aboard an Imperial Airways "Argosy" airliner during which Bill pointed out the capital's major landmarks.

On New Year's Day 1931 he was invited on an extensive tour of Germany as a guest of the national airline, Deutches Lufthansa. Shortly after arriving at Cologne Airport on the 2nd January he met Amy Johnson who was attempting to fly from Croydon to Moscow:

"Amy Johnson landed as she was unable to reach Berlin, so I looked after her until she flew off to Berlin the following day."

Later in the month he returned from Cologne to Croydon with Sabena. The cloudbase was very low, and approaching Dover Bill noted that they were flying at 50 feet below the top of the cliffs and that rockets had to be fired by the control staff at Croydon to help the pilot to locate the Aerodrome. He also flew aboard the new Handley Page 42 Airliner, G-AAGX, "Hannibal," just a week after the new aircraft entered service, to the opening of the new Plymouth Municipal Airport by the Prince of Wales. He was very impressed by the high level of comfort provided aboard this stately aircraft. His next flight in the HP 42 was five months later in "Horatius", with his old friend Walter Rogers, who gave him the controls during a flight to Paris, as did Jimmy Youell on the return journey. It seems almost unbelievable today that a non-flight crew member, even a former pilot, would be allowed to take the controls of an airliner on a public transport flight, but the conventions of the time were very different and it seems that it was quite normal practice for pilots to give their friends at Croydon a chance to take the controls when the opportunity arose.

The steady increase in traffic volumes at Croydon continued. Aircraft movements now frequently exceeded 100 a day during the summer months and the control tower staff were often called on to handle over 20 flights simultaneously at peak times. The frugal Air Ministry had no plans to increase the number of Aerodrome Control Officers working at Croydon, and Bill and his colleagues now had to handle an ever increasing workload, working long hours which often required an overnight stay between shifts in the special sleeping accommodation provided adjacent to the Control Tower. A former colleague of Bill's from the A.T.& T. days, Arthur Brenard, Press Officer at Imperial Airways, described a typical nights work for the Control Officers at Croydon during 1932 in an article entitled "Up in the Magic Tower":

"London's airport at Croydon is disgorging its thousands of employees and, to the homeward-bound motorist on the adjoining Brighton road, presents a serene if brilliantly illuminated spectacle.

"Closing for the day", is probably his comment, but in reality Croydon is just entering the biggest and most spectacular period of its daily adventures. In the masted Control Tower the stage is being set on a real live drama, where luck and chance are not even allowed in the wings. The night mail is leaving for Paris! If the heroine in distress is the airliner, and for and the Paris route's notorious weather are the villains, the role of the ever-ready and dashing hero must certainly be played, jointly by wireless and by Captain Lawford. In private life and in his off-duty moments on the aerodrome "Bill" Lawford is a popular, hearty men, full of civil and military flying reminiscences dating from the Hendon days, and has a fondness for any mechanical device which he invariably calls "gadgets".

In the night-mail drama, however, the "Bill" is dropped, and Captain Bill Lawford, AFC, becomes a tense figure, with iron-grey hair, alive to every development which the wonders of aerial science, housed in the tower, reveal to him. The night-mail pilot, Captain Willie Armstrong, requests weather reports for the route on which in a few minutes he is to pilot the night-mail plane, with some thirty souls on board. Wireless operators at Captain Lawford's elbow tap Morse keys and Captain Armstrong's requests are flashed across the Channel. A pause, and then the silence is broken by the replies from the principal points along the route. The pencil of the man at the keys races across his paper and a crazy jumble of numbers and letters appears;

"Le Bourget: cloud height 400 metres; visibility 800 metres. Beauvais: the same. A general slow improvement. (Wind) average 24 kilometres per hour. General direction North West"

All this and a lot more is read from these cryptic figures and letters, and the pilot is reassured.

"Going to be a little sticky Bill," he remarks to Lawford, "but nothing really to worry about. The wind on my tail will be a help anyway."'

Bill Lawford at work in the Croydon Control Tower
E.H. Lawford Archive

"All correct sir," he reports as the Commander comes aboard. A flick of Lawfords finger on the control panel in the tower and the whole landing area is illuminated.

Back in the tower "Bill" is transformed and becomes Captain Lawford.

"1830 hours' Paris liner requests permission to taxi out sir," he is informed by the look out man on the balcony of the tower. Permission is granted and the giant comes to life and takes up its position at the beginning of the beam of the million candlepower mobile searchlight.

"Paris liner in position for take-off," hails the look out man.

Lawford surveys the brilliantly illuminated landing area and makes a careful scrutiny of the route map in front of him.

"Let her go," he answers.

A confirming flash of light reaches the Commander's eye from the look out; the throttles are opened and the four engines whine their song of power. Faster and faster she races across the turf, her silver fuselage glinting in the beam of light and casting macabre shadows. She's off! The whine from the already invisible liner becomes a hum. The hum, a silence. The next direct contact with the earth is France.

Lawford is already in wireless communication with the plane, whose position on the air map in front of him is marked by a small flag bearing the letters "G-AAXD". That's its international registration mark," he explains. A few minutes later another flag appears on the map marked "G-AAXC".

That's "Heracles", the London bound liner from Paris," explains Lawford. "Left Paris on time, too, so we should be guiding him in about 8.45. The weather's none too good over the Channel. We shall have to see they don't get too near each other."

The activity in the tower is unceasing. The high - pitched buzz of Morse is occasionally interrupted by verbal requests, through a loudspeaker, from small aircraft that do not carry a skilled wireless operator. A message from "G-AAXD" reveals she is over the Channel and will soon be passing the French Coast. "G-AAXC" announces that she is approaching the English coast. Lawford determines the height of each aircraft and makes sure that there is ample margin for them to pass in safety at different heights and tracks.

"Le Bourget will take 'G-AAXD' over soon," Lawford explains, "and guide her by wireless on her last stage. All we've got to worry about, now, is guiding 'G-AAXC' across the Channel and keeping her clear of other aircraft."

The weather between the English coast and Croydon is deteriorating Clouds almost touching the ground completely obscure the lights of towns and aerial lighthouses from the view of the incoming night mail pilot. Only his wireless, in conjunction with the wonderful direction-finding equipment, can guide him safely to the airport.

"Now for the part that requires careful handling," this from Lawford, 'XC's' position please," he asks the operator.

"Just coming through," he is informed. " 'XC' reports position English coast Bexhill and entering a bank of low lying cloud." The wonderful direction-finder is brought into operation.

"A compass bearing for Croydon please," asks "G-AAXC", which is flying in thick cloud, so thick that its wing-tips are invisible to the passengers completing their dinners in the cabins. The liners wireless operator sends a signal which is picked up as a high-pitched hum by the tower. The tower operator twirls the knob on the direction-finding instrument, which controls an apparatus similar to a frame aerial. Then the hum is at its loudest note the frame aerial is pointing directly at the liner quick calculation by the operator and the required bearing is flashed to the liner flying sixty or seventy miles away.

At regular intervals the liner requests further bearings to check her course, the little flag on Lawford's map gets closer and closer to Croydon. Through the loudspeaker comes a voice, dulled by the roar of the engines;

"Hullo Croydon. Hullo Croydon. 'XC' calling. Understand am over Biggin Hill. Am preparing to land. Request bearing to Croydon. Over".

The switch is thrown over and the tower operator, after using the direction-finding instrument, verbally supplies a bearing calculated to bring the liner directly over the tower.

Outside the tower, winking orange lights reveal the boundaries of the 'drome. The mobile searchlight turns night into day along the path the rapidly approaching liner is to land,

Lawford is on the balcony of the tower now, cupping his ears for the first sound of the engines, the air of expectancy can almost be felt.

"Here she comes!" exclaims Bill suddenly, and the gentle hum of the engines is heard.

The hum grows into a deep-throated roar, which tells Lawford that the invisible liner is directly overhead.

"Nothing much wrong with our bearings," he says, justly proud of the Tower organisation.

"Inform 'XC' she's overhead," this to the wireless operator. The message is flashed to the liner and the roar dies away. Suddenly a green and a red light, which are the lights of the starboard and port wing tips, break through the cloud, making for the illuminated landing area.

A breathtaking moment as the huge liner is gracefully banked into the correct landing glide by the capable hands of its commander, and then, light as a feather, the huge 15 ton airliner makes contact with the earth. A short speed-reducing run, and the giant taxis onto the arrival platform.

In the tower Lawford runs over the completed log of the liners flight and surveys the positions of other aircraft in his zone. On the tarmac below, a huge German mail plane is waiting for the take-off signal, while almost simultaneously a sister liner is waiting to leave Berlin for Croydon. Captain

Lawford bends over his maps and pins the little flags that are air liners into position, and prepares to repeat the whole process. Croydon never sleeps"

During the summer season Bill attended many aviation events and Air Shows, often flying from Croydon to these events. On 4th June 1932 he flew to the Henly's Air Rally at Heston in the HP 42, "Horatius", with Walter Rogers and Jimmy Youell. Amy Johnson and her husband, Jim Mollison, were guests of honour and presented the prizes during the afternoon, while "Horatius" gave pleasure flights and the new Cierva Autogyro demonstrated it's novel flying capabilities.

On 20th May 1933 the Guild of Air Pilots and Navigators held their Annual Air Display at Brooklands. This event was attended by H.R.H. the Prince of Wales, who was greeted by the Deputy Master of the Guild, Capt. F.E. Guest following his arrival in the new Vickers Viastra. Unfortunatly the Display did not run according to schedule, and Bill, who was seated next to the Prince, had the task of keeping him updated on the changes to the various Display acts. Also with Bill at the Display were the Chief Test Pilot of Handley Page, Major Jim Cordes, and the well known aviatrix, the Duchess of Bedford, who was to lose her life four years later when she disappeared on a flight off the east coast of England.

The busy summer continued and Bill attended three more events during June, flying to the Household Brigade Military Flying Meeting at Heston on the 7th from Croydon in a Sabena Fokker F.VII. He also helped in the organisation of the Eastbourne Air Rally, flying down to Eastbourne in a Ford Tri-Motor. A Concours d'Elegance was held and the event was attended by many types ranging from the new Blackburn Monospar and deHavilland Dragon to the veteran Handley Page W10 now operated by Sir Alan Cobham for joyriding. The 26th saw Bill at the S.B.A.C. Show at Hendon, returning to Croydon aboard the Armstrong-Whitworth AW15 "Aurora" with Jimmy Youell and Anthony Fokker.

Following persistant requests to the Air Ministry for extra staff to relieve the workload of the four Control Officers at Croydon, Mr. A.L. Russell joined the Control Tower team on a temporary contract during the summer of 1933, allowing Bill to take his first extended period of leave for 18 months during July, when he made a return trip to India, flying out on the second Indian Air Mail service to leave Croydon. On the final leg of the sector from Allahabad to Calcutta, the Armstrong Whitworth 15, G-ABTK "Athena", flown by Capt. Mollard, sustained damage when it was forced to land at Asansole, and Bill had to make eight hour train journey to reach Calcutta. Fortunately another A.W.15, G-ABTL, "Astrea", flown by Capt. Brackley, had arrived at Calcutta returning from an extensive goodwill tour of Australia and the Far East, and Bill joined Brackley aboard this aircraft for the first leg of the return flight to Croydon.

The Guild of Air Pilots and Navigators Air Display at Brooklands, May 1933, from left to right, Jim Cordes, Test Pilot Handley Page Ltd., Bill Lawford, H.R.H. The Prince of Wales and the Duchess of Bedford

E.H. Lawford Archive

    From the start of regular airline operations "contact" flying at low altitude using prominent ground features had been the usual method of navigation used in bad weather conditions, but with the development of gyroscopic flight instruments and the installation of a radio beacon at Croydon pilots were now beginning the transition to the much safer practice of blind flying on instruments at a safe altitude. Scheduled airline traffic using Croydon had more than doubled during the year, and consequently, from November 1933, a Controlled Zone was brought into use whenever visibility was less than 100 yards or the cloudbase below 1000 feet, to protect commercial aircraft using the Airport from other traffic using the surrounding airspace. Aircraft were required to obtain permission from the Control Tower to enter this Zone for landing, which was granted on a strictly "first come first served basis". Bill and his colleagues were now working under to an ever increasing number of new written directives issued by the Chief C.A.T.O. at Croydon, Major Richards, and had been empowered to issue specific instructions to aircraft intending to enter the

Croydon Zone, a situation which often resulted in friction with the pilots who resented being instructed to remain clear of the new Zone and await their turn to land. Permission for aircraft on the ground to enter the landing and take-off area was given by a disc showing the initials of the airline company displayed from the balcony of the Control Tower, or by use of an Aldis signal lamp mounted on the corner of the Control Tower Balcony which directed a beam of white light at the waiting aircraft. If this light malfunctioned the ensuing delay to departing aircraft could cause problems which were depicted in a cartoon by the artist Richard Godfrey published in the spring of 1934 entitled "The Light That Failed",[13] depicting Bill standing on the Balcony of the Control Tower attempting to sort out the situation.

On 2nd March Bill flew with pilot "Bill" Bailey in the Puss Moth G-ABSO during a series of flights to test the new P.B. Gyro[14] stabilisation system, an early form of autopilot, and was very impressed, commenting that it was a *"remarkable system of gyroscopic control."*

1934 was another busy year for Bill, with further visits to airshows beginning on 24th May with a visit to the Empire Air Day Air Display at Eastbourne aboard the D.H. Dragon G-ACPY, piloted by Capt. Gordon Olley, where organised the air traffic control facilities for visiting aircraft.

On 16th July Bill made a second Broadcast for the B.B.C. This time it was a live outside broadcast from the Control Tower for "Children's Hour" with Derek McCullough, "Uncle Mac", an old R.F.C. colleague who had flown with Bill as an observer back in 1918. Bill received a fee of 5 guineas (£5.25), for this broadcast, and the "Radio Times" reported:

"This afternoon, Mac is going down to Croydon, and it is hoped that you will hear two or three aeroplanes actually take off and arrive. You are to hear Mac talk with one of the Control Tower officers. He will describe the scene and ask the officer questions and you will hear his answers. And what makes it all the more interesting is that during the war Mac used to sit in the aeroplane which this officer, E.H. "Bill" Lawford, flew. Mac was his observer then, and he is to be your observer now.

---

[13]Published in "Brooklands Track and Air", May 1934

[14]The PB Gyro equipment has survived and is on display at the Heritage Centre at Airport House, Croydon.

"THE LIGHT THAT FAILED"
(i.e. the taking off signal)

Bill Lawford stands on the balcony of the Control Tower surveying the chaos resulting from the failure of the signal lamp used to give permission for take-off situated at the near corner of the balcony. The operators of the light work frantically to repair the problem while the engines of the departing airliners awaiting clearance overheat. A Pekinese dog, "Minkey" is shown in Bill's pocket. This dog belonged to Bill's partner, Antoinette Hennington, and was a frequent visitor to the Control Tower. "Minkey" was often to be seen relieving herself out on the apron! She made her first flight aboard the massive Junkers G.38 during it's first visit to Croydon.

via Croydon Airport Society

Ten days later Bill attended a Luncheon at the Savoy Hotel, given by the Guild of Air Pilot's and Navigators, to honour the pioneer pilot Louis Bleriot on the 25th Anniversary of his first flight across the English Channel. This event was attended by many of the pioneers of British aviation and was followed by a the formal ceremony attended by the Honorary Wardens and members of the Court of the Guild to sign a Petition to the Privy Council for the grant of a Charter of Incorporation. Since being elected as a member in 1929, Bill had worked to promote the objectives of the Guild, and by 1934 he had been elected Assistant Treasurer, a position which he held for two years.

The Luncheon given by the Guild of Air Pilots and Navigators to honour Louis Bleriot on the 25th Anniversary of his historic crossing of the English Channel.

E.H. Lawford Archive

A further increase in air traffic at Croydon during 1934 resulted in an even heavier workload for the Duty Officers in the Control Tower. Jimmy Jeffs was now frequently absent setting up Radio and Control facilities at many of the new Municipal Aerodromes, and both John Morkham and Bill frequently took sick leave, probably due to the intense pressure that they were under working long hours in the Control Tower. Following representations from the Control Tower officers in November, the Air Ministry agreed to retain Mr. Russell on a permanent basis, and also employed a new officer, Mr. F.H. Robinson, bringing the number of qualified Aerodrome Officers at Croydon up to six.

At the end of 1936 Bill was transferred from Croydon to Lympne as Aerodrome Officer-in-Charge. H.W. Chattaway, his old friend and colleague from the A.T.&T. days, had unexpectedly resigned from his position as Deputy Chief Aerodrome Officer at Croydon after failing to be appointed as Chief Aerodrome Officer following the resignation of Major Richards. Chattaway left

Croydon for Singapore to take up a position in the Colonial Service, where tragically, he later committed suicide. Major Richards was succeeded as Chief Aerodrome Officer by Air Commodore E.H. Robinson, and Mr. R.C.I. Pearce, was taken on to bring the number of qualified Officers working in the Control Tower back up to six. The new domestic air services now operating from the Municipal Airports resulted in increased demand for qualified controllers which the Air Ministry was reluctant to satisfy from a limited civil aviation budget. However, the Maybury Report of 1936 recommended that the State should be responsible for Traffic Control and Communications at the Municipal Airports, and as a small number of newly trained control personnel were now becoming available, many of the original Aerodrome Officers at Croydon were now dispersed to the new provincial airports.

Psychic Experiences and the R.101 Disaster

Few families in Britain were left untouched by the huge loss of life during the Great War, and many harboured a strong desire to uncover the truth concerning the untimely death of loved ones in the conflict which lead to the formation of many groups engaged in psychic research, clairvoyancy and spiritualism during the 1920's. Following the early death of a much loved brother from pneumonia at only 39 years of age, Bill studied the work of W.T. Stead, the psychic researcher, well known spiritualist, and editor of the Pall Mall Gazette, who had sailed on the "Titanic" against the advice of a clairvoyant and was one of those to perish in the 1912 disaster. Bill studied the story of Stead's "Communications from the other side", and as early as 1928 he became convinced that communication with the deceased was possible. It might seem contradictory that a former pilot with a sound knowledge of physics working with the latest technical equipment at the most modern Airport of the time claimed to have experienced communications from beyond the grave, but the strange events which followed a series of tragedies that had claimed the lives of some of the most famous personalities in British civil aviation convinced Bill and others that there could be more behind these events than pure coincidence.

An old friend of Bill's, the much respected pilot Capt. Raymond Hinchliffe had disappeared in March 1928 while attempting to make the first non-stop east to west flight across the North Atlantic. Hinchliffe had flown for the Instone Airline, K.L.M. and Imperial Airways even though he had lost the sight of his left eye due to a wound received during the Great War and was one of the most experienced pilots of the time, but he now faced increasingly stiff medical examinations which made it likely that he would soon be grounded by his disability. Hinchliffe had long harboured an ambition to make the first flight across the North Atlantic from east to west, and his enthusiasm for the venture grew following Charles Lindberg's solo flight from New York to Paris the previous year. In a last gamble to provide for his wife and young family before his "B" Licence was withdrawn on medical grounds, Hinchliffe secured the sponsorship of one of Britain's richest heiresses, the publicity seeking Hon. Elsie McKay, daughter of Lord Inchcape, who would accompany him on his attempt on the North Atlantic. The flight was planned with the utmost secrecy, as had Lord Inchcape been aware of his daughter's intentions he would undoubtedly have tried to stop the venture. Hinchliffe was guaranteed a fee of £10,000, a considerable sum of money at the time, and Elsie McKay also agreed to take out an insurance policy for £10,000 on Hinchliffe's life to provide for his family in the event of his death.

Under great secrecy Hinchliffe and Elsie McKay took off in their Stinson Detroiter from R.A.F. Cranwell on 13th March 1928. The aircraft was observed passing Mizen Head, on the extreme south west tip of Ireland, some four hours later, but nothing further was seen or heard of the Stinson, and as time passed it was assumed that they had been lost in the vastness Atlantic Ocean. Later Hinchliffe's wife, Emilie, was shocked to discover that the promised insurance policy on her husband's life for £10,000 was void as Elsie McKay's cheque to cover the cost of the policy had bounced as there were insufficient funds in her bank account to cover the premium. Lord Inchcape ignored pleas to honour his daughter's promise to Hinchliffe, and bequeathed his daughter's substantial estate to the nation to help offset the national debt. Emilie Hinchliffe's work as a shorthand typist was now her only source of income to support her family.

A month after her husband's disappearance Emilie was contacted by a lady who claimed that Hinchliffe had "come through" to her with details of the last hours of the ill-fated flight during a seance held by the well known medium Eileen Garrett. Emilie, a down to earth Dutchwoman, was unconvinced, but after further persuasion agreed to attend a number of Mrs Garrett's seances during which she claimed that her late husband appeared, through the medium, to "communicate" many details of his last flight. Using her shorthand skills Emilie made extensive notes of many of the technical details revealed during these seances, during which it was claimed that Hinchliffe also enquired after old friends and colleagues including Bill Lawford and Capt. John Morkham. Morkham, a colleague of Bill's in the Control Tower at Croydon, was also an old friend of Ray and Emilie Hinchliffe. A mystified Emilie enlisted Morkham's help to verify the accuracy of much of the technical details revealed during the seances. Initially, Emilie Hinchliffe said nothing about her investigations, but following the resolution of her financial problems in the autumn of 1928 when Elsie McKay's promise was honoured by the Public Trustee Office making a grant of £10,000 to her, she revealed the story of the "communications" with her dead husband at a public presentation on the subject of her father's work on psychic phenomena organised by W.H.Stead's daughter at the Caxton Hall, London, on the 22nd November. The story generated enormous public interest and the presentation attracted a huge crowd of curious people filling the Hall to capacity with many being turned away.

In March 1928, seven months before the loss of Ray Hinchliffe and Elsie McKay, the Atlantic had claimed the life of another experienced and popular Croydon pilot, Col. Freddie Minchin, who also disappeared on an attempt to make an east to west crossing of the North Atlantic. The loss of these two highly respected pilots and the revelations of Emilie Hinchliffe had shaken many of the small band of experienced aviation professionals at Croydon, but it was now time to move on, and two weeks after Emilie Hinchliffe's revelations at Caxton Hall, a group of the most experienced pilots and navigators came together for the first annual "Veteran Air Navigators' Dinner,"[15] held on 5th December 1928 at Rules Restaurant, Maiden Lane, London. Bill was present at this gathering, which was chaired by Sqdn. Leader E.L. Johnston, a highly experienced navigator later to be appointed as Navigating Officer of the Government airship R.101, who stated in a speech that it was now time that the high standards achieved by the pioneers of civil aviation should be maintained by the formation of a new professional organisation. In his after dinner speech the D.C.A., Sir W. Sefton Brancker, suggested that there were the foundations of what could become a City of London Livery Company amongst those present, most of whom held a top professional qualification and had been involved in aviation for many years. Following the D.C.A's suggestion, all holders of an Air Ministry "B" Pilot's Licence or an Air Navigators Licence were invited to attend a meeting held at Rules Restaurant the following February, at which it was agreed to form a professional body to be known as "The Company of Air Pilots and Navigators of the British Empire", later changed to "The Guild of Air Pilots and Navigators" (G.A.P.A.N.). At the first meeting of the newly elected Foundation Council of the Guild held on 1st July 1929, Bill was elected as a Law Member of the new organisation.

Founder members of the Guild of Air Pilots and Navigators Lunch held at Rules Restaurant, 11th September 1930. At the head of the table is the first Master of the Guild, Sir W. Sefton Brancker with Sir Charles Kingsford-Smith to his left. Bill Lawford is seated fourth from the left.

Courtesy of GAPAN

---

[15] See Appendix 5, Documents, page 8

Evidence that Hinchliffe and Elsie McKay had perished the Atlantic Ocean appeared during February 1929, when a wheel from a Stinson Detroiter, identified from it's serial number as having been fitted to Hinchliffe's aircraft, was found on a beach in Co. Donegal, north-west Ireland. Bill Lawford's interest in the reports of the psychic events following the loss of his friend Hinchliffe had continued, but by the end of the year the main focus was now on the new airships which were being constructed to link the British Empire by air. On 14th October the Government sponsored Airship, R.101, made it's maiden flight, during which it flew overhead London, it's huge size bringing large crowds out on to the streets. The future possibilities of using airships commercially for long distance flights had been demonstrated as early as 1919 when the Government Airship R.34 flew non-stop from Scotland to New York and back. Commercial aircraft still lacked this kind of range, and the airship was seen as a practical means of linking Britain to the Empire by air. The Government had implemented an experimental development programme which lead to the construction of the private venture Airship, R.100, intended to serve the route between Britain and Canada, and the Government sponsored R.101 designed for the route to India. But major problems discovered during the initial test flights and damage sustained while riding out a gale at the Cardington Mooring Mast in November had resulted in unexpected delays to the programme, and the R.101 had to undergo a complete refit.

Emilie Hinchliffe continued to search for details of her husband's fate, and John Morkum continued to check the veracity of the technical details relating to his last flight which she had obtained during her sessions with Eileen Garrett. Morkum's interest grew and although he still remained sceptical, Emilie persuaded him to attend a number of seances with her during which Hinchliffe again "came through". Morkham too eventually became convinced that these "communications from beyond the grave" were real, as he believed that it was very unlikely that Eileen Garrett could have been aware of so many technical details which were known only to a few close friends who had been directly involved in the clandestine preparations for Hinchliffe's last flight. The information "communicated" by Hinchliffe now took a more sinister turn when, through Eileen Garrett, he warned of an impending disaster to the R.101 and urged Emilie to contact Sqn. Ldr. Johnston, the airship's Navigator. This Emilie did, but Johnston had great confidence in the airship programme and he remained unconvinced by Emilie's revelations. Emilie claimed to have received further warnings of a disaster which would befall the R.101 through Eileen Garrett, but realised that there was no point in passing them on to the sceptical Johnson. John Morkum however, aware of his colleague's interest in psychic research, told Bill about the *" the astounding facts"* revealed through Eileen Garrett concerning the R.101.

The R.101 emerged again from it's shed in late June 1930, making a further series of test flights during which it appeared overhead the RAF Pageant at Hendon, but a major problem remained as it had been calculated that there would be insufficient lift available for the airships's return flight through the heat of the Middle East to London, and the R.101 was returned again to it's shed at Cardington to have a new section accommodating extra gasbags inserted to provide the extra lift. The Secretary of State for Air, Lord Thompson, the architect of the airship programme, had made well publicised plans to travel to India on the maiden flight of the R.101, and to return to London in time for the conclusion of the Imperial Conference on the 20th October, with the aim of giving a convincing demonstration of the future potential of airships on the Empire routes. Little time for test flying remained following the completion of modifications to the R.101 at the end of September, and the Airship made only one test flight lasting almost 17 hours in excellent weather conditions, before leaving Cardington for India on the evening of the 5th October, carrying Lord Thompson and the D.C.A. Sir Sefton Brancker. Heading into worsening rain and gales and weighed down by a storm damaged and water saturated envelope, the

The burned out skeleton of the R.101 near Beauvais, October 1930

R.101 struck the ground near Beauvais, Northern France, seven and a half hours later. Immediately 5.5 million cubic feet of highly inflammable hydrogen gas exploded, incinerating most of the passengers and crew including Lord Thompson and Sir Sefton Brancker. Only 6 out of the of 54 souls aboard survived the explosion.

Croydon had continuously monitored the radio communications between the R.101 and it's base at Cardington and provided position checks on request. The last radio message from the R.101, requesting a position report, had been received by Croydon at 1.51 am, and was acknowledged at 01.52 am. At 2.18 am the airship called Croydon to say that no further assistance would be required and thanked them for their assistance. Bill was on duty in the Control Tower that night and he described the atmosphere:

"I was standby Duty Officer at the time, and when the awful news came through on the wireless we simply could not believe it. Nothing could be done but obtain the details as they filtered through to the Control Tower Wireless Department. It was the greatest shock that I have ever received - for days after the mental gloom over Croydon Airport was almost unbearable."

Two weeks after the disaster Bill flew to Paris in the cockpit of the Imperial Airways "Argosy", G-AACJ, with another old colleague, Capt. Arthur Wilcockson, taking the controls of the aircraft for most of the flight. The route to Paris passed near Beauvais and Bill made a low pass overhead the skeletal remains of the R.101 which still lay scattered around the crash site, remarking later that it was *"a terrible sight."* The tragic loss of life in the R.101 disaster including that of the much respected father figure of British civil aviation and first Master of the Guild of Air Pilots and Navigators, Sir Sefton Brancker, Bill's former boss during the A.T.&T. days, and the Deputy Master of the Guild, Sqdn. Ldr. Johnson, who had worked at Croydon during the summer of 1929, together with the loss of many other friends and colleagues, was a great blow to the close knit aviation community at Croydon Airport and would be felt for some time. The disaster resulted in the cancellation of the Airship Development Programme, but reports of further "psychic events" continued, including a report that the Commander of the R.101, H.C. Irwin, had "come through" and communicated many technical facts about the crash to a well known freelance journalist through the medium Eileen Garret a full year before publication of the official accident report. It was also reported that Brancker had visited an astrologer in 1925, and had been told that there was nothing to be seen in his life beyond the next six years. When Mrs Irwin was informed of her husbands death the day after the disaster she made the comment *"It's all right, I knew he wasn't coming back."*

Mindful of this and the details revealed during the Eileen Garrett seances which Morkham had recounted to him six months earlier, Bill continued to persue his interest in psychic phenomena and attended a series of seances conducted by another medium, Mrs Egerton, writing accounts of the seances that he had attended. Whether these seances were a series of carefully orchestrated confidence tricks is open to speculation, but many of those present were convinced that their experiences were genuine.

At an early seance with 10 or 11 other participants, the broad Irish voice of Larry, the guide, was heard through Mrs Egerton. Bill wrote:

Sound of aeroplane vibrations and Hinchliffe "came through":

"Of course I know him Longford[16] - Old Chap how is Millie[17] - have you seen her lately? The two children are grown women now. Here's power to your elbow Old Chap."

Sefton Branker is "coming through":

"Here we are - what!!! Have you read my book?[18] It's too thin, much more could have been included. Something is wrong with them (Air Authorities), they want some gunpowder under them.

Lawford:
"Things have gone wrong since you passed over - I wrote a eulogy about you in your book Old Chief."

Branker:
"Yes I know and I have come to thank you."

Lawford:
"What about Aircraft Transport and Travel, they were wonderful days."

Branker:
"What's wrong with Australia? Why do they buy American machines, they will find out one day. Now I want to tell you something, set your teeth can

---

[16]Lawford

[17]Hinchliffe's widow, Emilie

[18]"Sefton Branker" by Norman MacMillan, Heinemann 1935.

you. I am awfully sorry for your loss[19], you know what I mean, I know what it means to you. I was always one for the ladies what! (laugh). But I am deeply sympathetic and I know what it means to you.

Good fellow Morkham[20], the more you know of him the more you like him - but he keeps to himself too much and vegetates a lot."

There followed a lot of general metaphysical material from well known people who had passed over. During a further seance with Mrs Egerton on 30th December 1935, Branker "came through" again:

Branker:
"You know Lawford I was always one for the ladies - what about Egypt and India? - Things are very grave - references to 'my book' - They want a strong man down with you."

Lawford:
"You went across too soon Old Chief."

On 13th July 1936 Capt. Morkham accompanied Bill to another of Mrs. Egerton's seances which Bill described as follows:

"Larry, the Irish guide came through with the usual humorous remarks and references - a whole mass of messages from the departed came through to the various sitters who acknowledged the correctness of the signs. One lady had a conversation with her departed husband in the Malayan language, a most remarkable proof. Branker came through and spoke to Morkham and myself."

Brancker (to Morkham):

"Where is Villiers[21]? He used to call me "Brancks" and I used to quarrel with him. Do you remember N.E. Bray? He is just the same. Have you seen anything of "Auriol"[22] lately - she has written a new play (correct)

---

[19]Bill's long time partner, Antoinette Hennington, had recently died in August 1935 following a serious illness

[20]Capt. John P. Morkham, a colleague of Bill's in the Croydon Control Tower.

[21]Reference to Major Oliver Villiers, Air Ministry Intelligence Officer and assistant to Brancker.

[22]Auriol Lee was a London actress and playwrite who had been a friend of Brancker.

Brancker (to Lawford):
"What do you think of the "Hindenberg?"

Lawford:
"I saw her the other day when I was at Lympne."

Brancker:
"Yes, that's why I asked you[23], she's a wonderful airship after the thing we crashed in - that was a bad show.

Lawford:
"Do you think that we shall take up building them again?"

Brancker:
"Yes, they are bound to come as a practical proposition.

Lawford:
"What are the chances of war?"

Brancker:
"I think it is postponed for five years, if only we can muzzle Antony Eden, if you want peace."

Lawford:
"Do you think we should link up with the Germans?"

Brancker: (Emphatically)
"Of course we should to ensure World peace - I often come up in your old 'Conning Tower'."

Lawford:
"You told me last time that Australia was buying American aircraft."

Brancker:
"Yes. Why cannot they be patriotic and buy ours?"[24] He then spoke about Auriol Lee and continued: "I was a great one with the ladies - What, a ladies man, What! Good Bye."

---

[23] Bill considered this to be a "proof" as how could the medium have known this fact?

Later Hinchliffe "came through" and had a general talk with John Morkham and Bill saying that he had been very busy on important work. He then talked generally about his children and wife and Millie's marriage which would provide a nice home for the children, also other private domestic matters known only to a few personal friends.

Lawford:
"I've read your book Hinch."

Hinchliffe:
"It wasn't really I that wrote it[25]."

Bill then described the rest of the seance:

"After a lot of generalisms, during which we asked him why he did not come in his 'plane, he said something I cannot remember about 'vibrations' and then departed. The whole seance room then began to vibrate tremendously with his 'plane and engines and this went on for some minutes, most astonishing, everybody felt the vibrations intensely - this manifestation alone is a tremendous proof. After more sitters had received messages, Mr. Deacon went in to a trance and Sir William Crookes[26] "came through" and in a calm and beautifully serene voice likened communication to pure water passing through a dirty pipe so that water flowing out would be slightly contaminated - this is the analogy with imperfect mediumship - the evidence gets slightly distorted - the more perfect the medium the more perfect the evidence - which is obvious logic. He thanked the lady sitting next to me who is his writing medium for her perfect work. Close of seance.

During the seance I could distinctly see a goldish yellow aura around my body and see my hands and fingers as I moved them to and fro and opened and closed them. Capt. Morkham twice remarked simultaneously with myself of seeing a large blue star off the right side of the forehead (temple), many other small blue psychic stars were visible and the usual grey ectoplasmic mass in the

---

[24] Bill noted that this was evidential as he did not know of this before Brancker 'told him' at the previous seance but had since verified this fact.

[25] Bill noted that this referred to the collaboration of John Morkham and Emilie Hinchliffe in the compilation of Hinchliffe's biography.

[26] The nineteenth century psychic researcher Sir William Crookes.

centre and around Mrs. Egerton with a cold wind at times. I could also see a shadowy form over my right shoulder - but it was too indistinct."

Hinchliffe "came through" to Bill once more during a seance with Mrs. Egerton in April 1937, Bill wrote:

"Hinchliffe came, and said:

'you have been wonderful Bill, the only one that can make Mrs. Morkham unbend - I suppose it's your benign countenance and persuasive way. Have you seen Millie? Wasn't it awful, you know it makes me glad to know that she is married again, how are the children?' "

Genuine or not, these psychic session convinced Bill that communication beyond from the grave was possible, and as part of his attempts to make contact with those close to him who had "passed over" into the spirit world he attended many more sessions with different mediums and clairvoyants over the next few years.

World War Two and Retirement

By the mid 1930's the small team of control officers at Croydon were struggling to keep up with the rapidly increasing number of aircraft movements brought about by the growing popularity of air travel. Extra qualified control officers were urgently needed, but as the overworked Control Tower staff at Croydon had no time to provide training facilities for new recruits a training school was set up to train new controllers under the guidance of "Jimmy" Jeffs. When a limited number of newly trained control officers became available many of the "old hands" at Croydon were transferred to the new provincial airports to implement the operation of radio and traffic control systems.

Commander Deacon, the Air Ministry Officer-in-Charge at Lympne Airport for many years, retired at the end of 1936, and Bill was appointed to fill the vacant position. He was already very familiar with Lympne, having landed there many times during his flying days with A.T.& T. and had also worked there during temporary assignments from Croydon. Lympne was a tranquil backwater compared to Croydon. Heston and Gatwick airports had replaced Lympne as the preferred diversionary airports for Croydon, but the airport remained available as a diversionary aerodrome for cross-Channel flights when bad weather in the London area closed Heston and Gatwick and provided Customs facilities for light aircraft flying between the Continent and the U.K, and still acted as an important component of the Air Ministry radio-direction finding service, providing radio bearings to aircraft on request.

Many well known aviators arrived and departed from Lympne on record breaking flights during Bill's time there including Harold F.Broadbent, who left Australia on 27th April 1937 in Leopard Moth ,VH-AHB, arriving at Lympne six days later to claim the Australia to U.K. solo record. But Broadbent's record did not stand for long. On 24th October Jean Batten landed at Lympne in her Percival Gull Six, G-ADPR, after flying from Darwin in 5 days, 18 hours and 15 minutes, beating Broadbent's record. Bill was one of those who had the honour of carrying the exhausted New Zealand aviatrix shoulder high from her aircraft to the administration buildings. As Royal Aero Club Observer at Lympne, Bill officially recorded the arrival and departure of record breaking flights during his time at the airport.

Due largely to the efforts of W.E. Bill Davis, CFI of the Cinque Ports Flying Club, and his wife Ann, an International Air Rally was held annually at Lympne and Bill and his colleagues were kept busy handling large numbers of visiting aircraft from home and abroad. Social events were always a feature of this Rally, such as the Great Barbeque and Supper Dance for 500 guests organised by the Davis's during the Fifth International Air Rally held in late August 1937. Tragically, W.E. Bill Davis lost his life at Lympne while taking off the following spring in the Cinque Ports Flying Club's Blackburn ST4 Monospar, but his efforts and those of his wife had done much to promote interest in regular international aviation meetings. The Sixth International Air Rally was held at Lympne in 1938 and provided a nostalgic moment for Bill when a 1912 Caudron biplane, similar to the aircraft in which he had gained his R.Ae.C. Aviatiors Certificate back in 1913, arrived at Lympne from France on a delivery flight for preservation by the Nash Collection.

The Aerodrome Officers in the field acted as the eyes and ears of the Air Ministry and had now been granted considerable powers which included deputising for Customs, Immigration and C.I.D. if required. Bill's Air Ministry Authority, issued in June 1938 under the Air Navigation Orders, authorised him to enter and inspect any aerodrome or any place where aircraft requiring the grant of a Certificate of Airworthiness were being constructed and to detain and inspect aircraft and examine their documentation, draconian powers indeed.

Bill placed Lympne on full alert when the Imperial Airways H.P. 42, G-AAXD, "Horatius" made an emergency landing with a damaged undercarriage which collapsed on landing in September 1938. Luckily both crew and passengers were unhurt, and "Horatius" was repaired in one of Lympne's large hangars and returned to service.

On 17th May 1939 Bill gave up his long batchelorhood when he married Miss Arline King at the church of St. Stephen, Lympne. Following the ceremony an aircraft from the Cinque Ports Flying Club flew over the church and dipped in salute to the wedding party. But only a month later the aviation community at Lympne was shocked by the death of the popular aircraft designer Nick Comper. Comper was on a business visit to Lympne when a passer-by outside his hotel at Hythe mistook him for an IRA subversive and assaulted Comper who fell to the ground, striking his head on the kerb with fatal consequences.

War clouds were now gathering again, and in preparation for the seemingly inevitable conflict the Royal Navy Fleet Air Arm arrived at Lympne during July 1939. Civil air traffic within the British Isles continued to show a rapid increase with all the main airports reporting large increases in traffic volume. On 5th August, the last major air race to be held in Britain before the outbreak of War, the Folkestone Aero Trophy, was held at Lympne, attended by a large crowd of spectators.

In preparation for the outbreak of war all the Air Ministry Aerodrome Officers had been issued with sealed orders which were only to be opened on receipt of a secret code word from the Air Ministry. At 00.13 hours on 1st September 1939 Bill received this code word, "Bittersweet," by telephone and opened his sealed orders which instructed him to proceed immediately to the Channel Island of Jersey on secret war duties.

Bill was posted to Jersey to act as Base Censor and Cypher Officer on behalf of the Air Ministry at Jersey Airport, liaising with an old R.F.C. comrade, Charles Roche, Airport Controller for the States of Jersey, and Jack Herbert, Assistant Overseer at the Airport.

The initial apprehension which followed Chamberlain's announcement on 3rd September 1939 that *"this Country is at war with Germany,"* soon gave way to the complacency of the "Phoney War" which would last until the following spring. All civil flying had been prohibited over the eastern half of England, but a limited air service between the Channel Islands and the mainland recommenced on 24th October when Channel Island Airways began a service between Jersey and Shoreham Airport. That autumn saw the demise of Imperial Airways which was merged with British Airways to form the British Overseas Airways Corporation, (B.O.A.C.).

Life on Jersey continued virtually unchanged during the early months of the War, and over Easter 1940 there was the usual influx of visitors by air to the island and plans were afoot to increase the number of flights between the island and the mainland during the summer months to cater for the expected seasonal increase in visitor numbers.

The question of the wartime status of the Airport was raised on 11th June when a Squadron of R.A.F. Whitley bombers heading south for a raid on Northern Italy landed at Jersey to refuel. The States of Jersey authorities were unprepared and requested that the R.A.F provide extra men and equipment to handle future operations by R.A.F. aircraft, proposing that if Jersey was to be used on a regular basis by the R.A.F. the Air Ministry should consider taking over responsibility for the operation of the Airport from the States of Jersey.

Before this situation could be resolved the German invasion of the Low Countries and France and the rapid advance of the panzer divisions westwards towards Normandy during May 1940 caught those on the Channel Islands by surprise. Jersey Airport had now become a staging post for R.A.F. and civil aircraft engaged in the evacuation of British personnel from Western France. On 16th June, Louis Strange, an old colleague of Bill's from the pioneering days at Hendon, landed at Jersey Airport in a heavily loaded DH 84 "Dragon" to refuel. Strange had been engaged in the hurried evacuation of R.A.F. personnel and their belongings from Nantes ahead of the German advance, and had encountered enemy ground fire as he flew over Caen and Rennes. He was in no doubt about the gravity of the situation:

"I and my crew and passengers were all very tired, unshaven and dirty, and were no less astonished to find parties having tea in their Sunday best clothes, out on the verandah of the airport under bright coloured sunshades, than they were to see such a dishevelled crew from an R.A.F. aircraft. I went up to the control tower and told my old friend Bill Lawford that I thought it was time that they called it a day and packed up and got back to England. But no one would believe things were as bad as I made out. Within the next few hours they knew however, and 24 Squadron was able to help many to get away."[27]

---

[27]Typescript *More Recollections of an Airman,* by Louis A. Strange,

The regular air service operated between Jersey and Shoreham by Channel Island Airways had ceased the previous day, and this company now set about the task of evacuating those wishing to leave for England, assisted by aircraft from No. 24 Squadron R.A.F. The next day my mother and I became part of this aerial evacuation which would fly more than 300 people from Jersey to the mainland during the next few days. At just six weeks old this was my baptism of the air. General de Gaulle also landed at the Airport on the 18th aboard a DH Flamingo for refuelling, en-route from Bordeaux to Hendon.

Panic was now beginning to set in on Jersey, the French Government was seeking surrender terms from the Germans and soon France would capitulate and the German occupation of the Channel Islands would begin. Jack Herbert remained on Jersey during the occupation and later recalled that in the rush to evacuate as many as possible there was no time to weigh the passenger baggage, which was loaded aboard the aircraft at the discretion of the pilot. The Lawford family Ford "Anglia" had been left on the quayside at St. Helier Harbour packed with household effects, but it's contents were looted before it could be loaded for shipment to the mainland. A Squadron of R.A.F. Hurricanes had also arrived and was operating from the Airport to provide air cover for the evacuation of the B.E.F. from Cherbourg. On 18th June Bill received orders from the Air Ministry to return to the mainland and he flew out of Jersey to Heston aboard an aircraft of 24 Squadron. The last R.A.F aircraft flew out of Jersey in the early morning of 21st June. Later it was announced that Jersey, together with the other Channel Islands, was to be demilitarised to avoid the loss of life and property damage which would occur if attempts were made to repel a German attack. Bill's old friend and colleague Charles Roche remained on the island to manage the Airport on behalf of the States of Jersey, and was present on 1st July when the first Luftwaffe aircraft arrived at the Airport carrying a party of German officers to accept the surrender of the island to the forces of the Third Reich.

On his return to the mainland Bill was posted to Gatwick Airport as Air Ministry Officer-in-Charge. Following the declaration of war Gatwick had been requisitioned by R.A.F. Kenley, but as the newly formed B.O.A.C. required an operational base and overhaul facility to the south of London it had been agreed to transfer the Airport to the control of Air Ministry's Civil Aviation branch, provided that the B.O.A.C. agreed to vacate the the Airport within 24 hours on request. The chaotic situation following the evacuation of the B.E.F from Dunkirk and the fall of France had forced the abandonment of plans to re-start air services between England the near continent, and there was now a growing R.A.F. presence at Gatwick which provided a temporary refuge for aircraft escaping from France ahead of the German advance.

On Sunday 25th August 1940 British Air Transport came of age. The Battle of Britain raged in the skies above Gatwick, but the Airport played little part in the conflict. Even with the main news focussing on the hard pressed

R.A.F's defence of southern England, many of the newspapers still found space to comment on the progress of air transport during the 21 years that had elapsed since Bill had made the first flight of the regular service from Hounslow to LeBourget. The "Sunday Times" commented:

" In the twenty-one years of commercial flying the two-passenger converted bombers of that pioneer trip had grown to the 40 passenger giant which gave something approaching luxury in it's accommodation. The modest 100 mph cruising speed had been more than doubled............

But for the War, the twenty-first birthday of a mode of transport which will revolutionise the world's communications would have been a cause for celebration. Now it is passing almost unnoticed while the remnants of British commercial air transport struggle to maintain themselves on somewhat precarious routes."

B.O.A.C. relocated it's London operations to Heston, and by the end of 1940, only a token civil presence remained at Gatwick which was now home to the Westland Lysanders of No. 26 Army Co-Operation Squadron and the Boulton-Paul Defiants of No 141 Squadron. As the final withdrawal of B.O.A.C. from Gatwick had resulted in an almost total cessation of civil aviation activities at Gatwick and Bill was now sent north to a new posting at Barton Aerodrome, near Manchester.

Bill spent the rest of the War serving as an Aerodrome Officer at Barton Aerodrome and later at Bristol (Whitchurch) aerodrome, where he was responsible for supervising the small number of officially authorised civil aircraft movements. He had been granted a Commission in the R.A.F. Volunteer Reserve for the duration of hostilities, and also served as an Air Training Corps technical instructor with No.1477 Squadron at Barton and No.1009 Squadron at Bristol.

The small grass aerodrome Barton had served as the Municipal Airport for Manchester, but on the outbreak of war it was requisitioned for use by National Air Communications and a number of small air taxi companies, including Wrightways and Air Taxis Ltd. which had transferred there from their pre-war bases to operate military communications flights under special permit. These companies were also engaged in aircraft and engine repair work for the R.A.F. at Barton, mainly on Avro Ansons. The aerodrome had also been designated as the U.K. terminal for the regular air service to Dublin operated by the DH86B "Express Airliners" of West Coast Air Services Ltd and the Irish operator, Aer Lingus, but this service was transferred to Speke Aerodrome, Liverpool, during 1942. As the War progressed new hangars were built at Barton to facilitate the repair, assembly and air testing of many military types including, Fulmars, Hurricanes and Corsairs. The control of the aerodrome was transferred from National Air Communications to the Ministry of Aircraft

Production which resulted in a decline in civil air traffic movements, and in the spring of 1943 Bill was moved again to become Aerodrome Officer-in-Charge at Whitchurch Aerodrome, Bristol. Whitchurch was another Municipal Aerodrome which had been requisitioned by the Air Ministry on the outbreak of War. It remained a civil airport of entry for the duration of hostilities, handling flights operating under great secrecy carrying statesmen, military top-brass, film stars and other V.I.P.'s to Lisbon in neutral Portugal and also to Eire, from where an onwards connection by flying boat to Canada and the U.S.A. operated from Foynes on the Shannon estuary. The build-up for D-Day was now gathering pace and large numbers of American servicemen were now temporarily stationed in the Bristol area. Two U.S. Army officers were billeted with my family at this time. These kind men were more than generous, and my mother was occasionally presented with extra "goodies" obtained from the PX. I remember enjoying my first ever "Mars Bar" courtesy of these generous men who remained in contact with my parents long after the war was over.

In the midst of the wartime austerity, when the first V.1 "Doodlebugs" were falling on London, B.O.A.C. celebrated the 25th Anniversary of the start of British airline operations with a luncheon held on 25th August 1944 at the Dorchester Hotel, presided over by the Corporation's Chairman, The Viscount Knollys, which was attended by many of the airline pioneers of 1919. A telegram of congratulation from the King was read, and in his speech, a shrewd Lord Brabazon of Tara, holder of Aviators Certificate No.1, warned that the authorities in Britain had better wake up to the fact that the American air transport industry was now the most advanced in the world. Bill also spoke at this luncheon, and recalled the difficulties encountered by the first airline pioneers 25 years before.

With the end of World War 2 came retirement, and Bill retired from the Air Ministry on the 31st December 1945, returning to live in Jersey. The scars left by the German occupation of the island were still much in evidence and German P.O.W's were still engaged in dismantling many of the fortifications and military installations which had been constructed during the occupation.

Even in retirement he retained a strong interest in aviation developments, and in particular the experimental "Flying Wing" type aircraft such as the Armstrong Whitworth AW52 and the Northrop XB35 which were being evaluated at the time. He had never forgotten the inherently stable Dunne Tailess swept wing biplane which had flown at Hendon before the first World War, commenting that *"I always knew the flying wing would appear some day and my opinion has been justified."*

This prompted Bill to carry out experiments with a series of simple swept-wing model gliders consisting of two sheets of thin balsa wood joined together by a central pivot. By adjusting the angle of the balsa wood sheets forming the wings an extremely flat glide could be obtained. These model

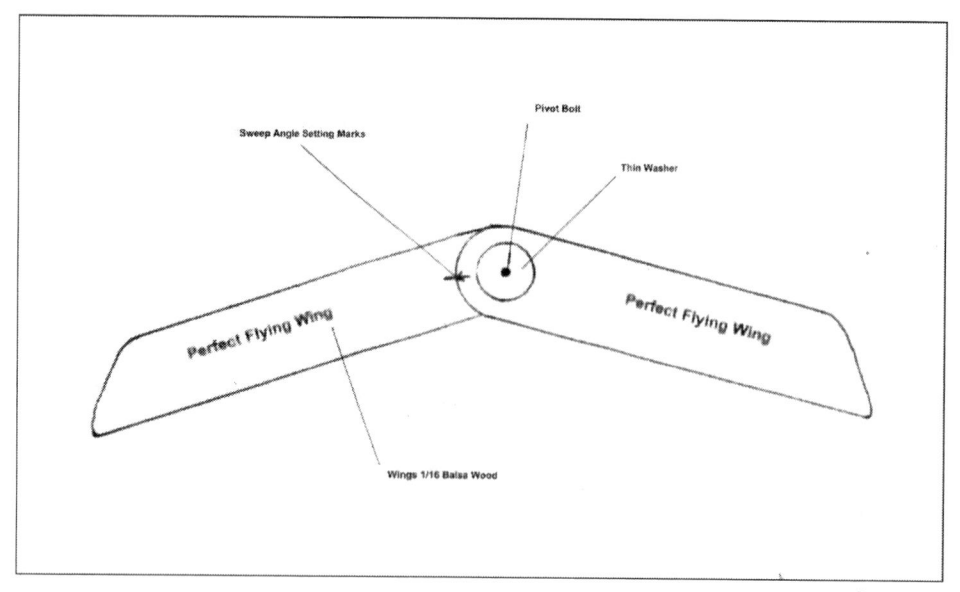

The simple Flying Wing model glider designed by Bill Lawford in 1949

gliders were easily carried with the wings folded together, and were constructed in various sizes, with wingspans from varying from 18" to over six feet. Some were fitted with a "Jetex" engine, and I remember seeing more than one climbing away under "Jetex" power only to disappear from view, never to be seen again. Bill hoped to market these models and had applied for a provisional Patent, but the austerity of the post war years forced him to drop these plans as he was unable to obtain supplies of suitable balsa wood to manufacture them in quantity.

The thirtieth anniversary of the British airline industry was marked on 25th August 1949 when a special luncheon was given for the pioneers of air transport by British European Airways at their temporary base at Northolt Airport. Bill was a Guest of Honour at this function, which was attended by the Chairman and executives of B.E.A. and B.O.A.C., the Minister of Aviation, Lord Packenham, Sir Frederick Handley-Page and many old friends and colleagues from the pioneering days. Bill recalled the early days with a short speech:

"In 1919 the passengers were shepherded through the mud to board the aircraft, their luggage placed on their laps, and when all was set the lid of the cabin was shut down on top of them. The pilots often argued about which trip and route they should take. One would decide that it was his turn to go to Brussels, having already flown four services to Paris that week. The fact that I had done a good deal of flying over northern France during the War helped me

to navigate through the bad weather with no radio or navigation aids on that first flight of the service".

Underlining the huge progress made by the airline industry over the previous thirty years it was announced by the Chairman of B.E.A., Lord Douglas of Kirtleside, himself a pioneer airline pilot and formerly Chief Pilot of Handley Page Air Transport back in 1919, that B.E.A. had made a profit for the first time and had placed an order for the new Vickers Viscount 700 turbo-prop airliner, the prototype of which was parked outside on the Northolt apron together with the elegant Airspeed Ambassador and the new small four engined Miles Marathon feederliner, and that it was planned that the Ambassador would be in service by 1951. Unfortunately, the planned demonstration flights by these aircraft had to be cancelled due to poor visibility in the London Control Zone.

From converted First World War bombers to the first Turbo-Prop airliner - celebrating the 30th Anniversary of the British Airline Industry at Northolt in front of the Vickers Viscount 700 prototype, from left to right:

Commandant. E.J.Bouderie, Air Union, Capt. H. "Jerry Shaw", A.T.&T., Capt. Walter Hope, Imperial Airways, Capt. A.S. Wilcockson, H.P. Air Transport & B.O.A.C., Capt. Bill Lawford, Lord Douglas of Kirtleside, H.P. Air Transport and Chairman, B.E.A., Capt. Gordon Olley, Imperial and Olley Airways, Sir Miles Thomas, Chairman, B.O.A.C., and Wing.Cdr. H.M.D. Walker, DeHavilland Aircraft Co.
Courtesy of the Flight Collection

This was to be Bill's last re-union with many of his old aviation friends and colleagues from the early days of British air transport. In 1951 he moved from Jersey to live at Bexhill-on-Sea on the Sussex coast, where, after suffering a series of serious strokes, he passed away on 14th September 1955.

His obituary in the Royal Aero Club Gazette stated:

"Bill Lawford has a secure niche in fame as the pilot of the first airliner on the first British regular airline service."

The famous veteran airline pilot, Capt O.P. Jones, who, following a long and illustrious career, had recently retired as Chief Pilot of B.O.A.C., recalled:

"in the old days at Croydon Bill was a landmark and the friend of everyone."

He is laid to rest close by Gatwick Airport, within earshot of the arriving and departing airliners of the industry which he had helped to pioneer. On his headstone is inscribed the R.A.F. motto:

"Per Ardua ad Astra"

"Through Hardship to the Stars"

Appendix 1

The Aircraft Transport and Travel Traffic Book

This is an important record of the flights operated by Aircraft Transport and Travel Ltd. between 23rd August and 22nd April 1920, and is one of the few original company documents to have survived. This was due to the foresight of Mr.P.T.Griffith, an employee of of Ogilvie and Partners, the technical managers to the Instone Airline in the early 1920's, who had an office at Croydon Airport (Plough Lane). Instones had continued to use the Traffic Book to record their flights from 21st March until 31st August 1921. On the formation of Imperial Airways in 1924 Mr Eskell, Instone's Traffic Manager, was clearing out his office and presented the Traffic Book to Mr.Griffith as a momento of his time at Croydon. Griffiths kept the Traffic Book safe for nearly 50 years before disposing of it on his retirement to his then employers, B.O.A.C. It now forms part of the British Airways archives, and is presently held at the R.A.F. Museum, Hendon.

A page from the Aircraft Transport & Travel Ltd. Traffic Book showing the flights operated during the first few days of the London - Paris Service

The A.T.&T. Traffic Book has accepted as an accurate record of flights operated by A.T.&T, but comparison with other documents and stated facts reveals a number of discrepancies, especially regarding timings, so it's absolute accuracy can be drawn into question. For instance it is worth querying why all departures from LeBourget during the first week's operations are recorded as having departed on time at 12:30 pm, whereas departures from Hounslow are shown at varying times, often delayed, as might be expected. This indicates that the record keeper probably assumed a 12:30 pm departure time from LeBourget, recording the actual arrival times at Hounslow, which do vary. Arrival times at LeBourget are unrecorded after the first day of the service, indicating that this information was probably unavailable to the writer at Hounslow, as were the actual departure times from Paris.

Perhaps the most notable discrepancy is the in the recorded departure and arrival times of the Airco 16, K 130, for the first day of the London – Paris service on 25th August 1919, which are recorded as approximately 30 minutes earlier than the times stated by Bruce Ingram and subsequently reported in the following day's newspapers.

Comparison of the departure and arrival times given in the Traffic Book with the Personal Flying Logbooks of Bill Lawford and Jerry Shaw suggest that the departure times given in the Traffic Book are "Off Blocks", whereas the pilots logged their actual "Airborne" times, which may have been the practice at the time.

Flights operated by Aircraft Transport & Travel Ltd. are recorded until 22nd April 1920. There is then a break until 21st March 1921, when the Traffic Book was used by the Instone Airway to record their flights up to 31st August 1921.

Appendix 2

Logbooks

Bill Lawford's Logbook showing the entry for 25th August 1919

Jerry Shaw's Log Book for the first week of the London –Paris Service

Appendix 3

Aircraft operated by Aircraft Transport & Travel Ltd

Airco DH 4a

Rolls-Royce Eagle VIII Engine, 360 hp

Specifications and Performance

Cabin Biplane	Payload: 2 passengers or freight
Wing Span 42' 4"	Maximum Speed: 130 mph
Length 29'6"	Cruising Speed: 100 mph
Range: 438 statute miles	Climb to 10,000': 12 minutes
Empty Weight: 2,600 lbs	Max. A.U.W: 3,720 lbs

G-EAHF

Previously F2699
Acquired July 1919
C of R 5 Aug 1919
C of A 12 Aug 1919

Built by the Glendower Aircraft Co. as DH 4. Converted to DH 4A by Airco. this was the first of A.T.&T.'s DH4A's. Initially the aircraft retained R.A.F. serials until civil registration in early August. On 10th November 1919 this aircraft operated the first London – Paris Air Mail Flight. G-EAHF was written-off on 11th December 1919 following a fatal crash in poor visibility at Coulsdon

G-EAHG

Previously   F2694
Acquired   5 Aug 1919
C of R   5 Aug 1919
C of A   12 Aug 1919

Built by Glendower Aircraft Co as DH 4. Converted to DH 4A by Airco. Flown to the E.L.T.A Exhibition on 12 August 1919 by Capt. H.J. Saint. Departed for Switverland on sales tour, 24 September 1919. Ditched in Channel and written-off 29 Oct 1919.

G-EAJC

Previously   F2702
Acquired   Aug 1919
C of R   7 Aug 1919
C of A   19 Aug 1919

Built by Glendower Aircraft Co. as DH 4. Converted to DH4A by Airco. First Flight of Regular Civilian Continental Service from London to Paris, 25 August 1919. C. of A. expired 18 August 1920 and withdrawn from use. Sold November 1920.

G-EAJD

Previously   F2704
Acquired   Aug 1919
C of R   7 Aug 1919
C of A   22 Aug 1919

Built by Glendower Aircraft Co. as DH 4. Converted to DH 4A by Airco. Flew last scheduled service operated by the type on the London – Paris route on 8 January 1920. C. of A. expired 21 August 1920, withdrawn from use. Sold November 1920

Airco DH 9

Armstrong Siddley Puma Engine, 230 hp

Specifications and Performance

Open Cockpit Biplane
Wing Span 42' 5"
Length 30'10"
Range: 560 statute miles
Empty Weight: 2,755 lbs

Payload: 2 passengers or 600 lbs
Maximum Speed: 115 mph
Cruising Speed: 100 mph
Climb to 10,000': 18 minutes
Max. A.U.W: 3,300 lbs

G-EAAA

Previously: C6054

Acquired April 1919. Capt. H.J. Saint departed from Hendon for Bournemouth carrying newspapers for the Daily Mail in the early hours of 1 May 1919, but crashed in poor weather at Portsdown Hill and was written-off.

G-EAAC "Antopia"

Previously: **K 109**

H 9277

Acquired May 1919. Operated first international civil charter flight between Hendon and LeBourget flown by Lieut. Shaw on 15 July 1919. Sold to the deHavilland School of Flying, and later converted to a DH9J (Bristol Jupiter engine). Withdrawn from use 28 January 1933 and dismantled.

G-EAGX "Ancuba"

Acquired July 1919. Operated first scheduled service from London to Paris, 25 August 1919 (Lieut McMullin). Crashed September 1920.

G-EAGY

Previously: H 9258

Acquired July 1919 and flown that month to the ELTA Exhibition, (Lieut. Lawford). Sold abroad, April 1921

G-EALJ

Previously: D2884

Acquired 26th August 1919. Civil conversion probably abandoned, registration cancelled July 1920.

G-EAMX

Previously: D 5662

Acquired 15 September 1919. Flew on Hounslow – Amsterdam route for K.L.M. Sold to S.N.E.T.A, Belgium, April 1920

G-EAOP

Previously: H 5579

Acquired 20 October 1919. Written-off September 1920.

G-EAOZ

Previously: H 5889

c/n P.32E

Acquired October 1919. Made flight over 1920 Boat Race for Daily Telegraph. C of A expired July 1920. Sold to K.L.M November 1920 as H-NABF. Written-off 1924.

G-EAPL

Previously: H 5890

c/n P.33E

Acquired November 1919. November 1920, sold to K.L.M.as H-NABE. Written-off 30 May 1922.

G-EAPO

c/n P.34E

Acquired November 1919. Written-off September 1920

G-EAPU

"Acanthus"

c/n P.35E

Acquired November 1919. Fown by Lieut. McMullin on a sales trip to Warsaw and Prague on a sales trip during January and February 1920. Written-off, November 1920

G-EAQA

c/n P.36E

Acquired December 1919. Crashed January 1921.

G-EAQL

c/n P.38E

Acquired December 1919. Sold to K.L.M, January 1921.

G-EAQM

Previously: F1287

Acquired January 1920. Departed from Hounslow on 8 January and completed the first single engine flight to Australia.

G-EAQN

c/n P.37E

Acquired January 1920. Crashed December 1920

G-EAQP

c/n P.39E

Acquired January 1920. Chartered to K.L.M, 1920. Later operated in Newfoundland during 1922 by the Aerial Survey Co. in A.T.&T. markings

Airco 16

Rolls-Royce Eagle VIII Engine 360 hp

Specifications and Performance

Cabin Biplane
Wing Span: 46' 6"
Length: 31' 10"
Range: 358 statute miles
Empty Weight: 2,963 lbs

Payload: 4 Passengers or 720 lbs
Maximum Speed: 130 mph
Cruising Speed: 115 mph

Max. A.U.W: 4.378 lbs

G-EACT

Previously: K130

c/n DH 16/1

C of A 25 May 1919

Prototype DH 16, acquired May 1919. Operated first London – Paris scheduled service, 25 August 1919. Crashed into the sea off Brighton, 18 March 1920

G-EALM

c/n 4

C of A 9 September 1919

Acquired August 1919. Sold to the DeHavilland Hire Service, August 1922. Crashed at Stanmore, 10 January 1923.

G-EAPM "Agincourt"
c/n P.2
C of A 8 December 1919

Acquired November 1919.l Sold to deHavilland Hire Service 1922. C.of A. lapsed, scrapped November 1923.

G-EALU "Arras"
c/n P.1
C of A 22 September 1919

Acquired 22 September 1919. Used for airborne radio tests, January 1920. Operated first London – Amsterdam service for K.L.M, 17 May 1920. Cof A lapsed, scrapped November 1923.

G-EAPT
c/n P.3
C of A 8 December 1919

Acquired November 1919. Sold to deHavilland Hire Service, July 1922. Scrapped 6 July 1923.

G-EAQG
c/n P.4
C of A 24 January 1920

Acquired January 1920. Sold to River Plate Aviation Co, Argentina as R-137, April 1920

Airco 16

Napier Lion Engine, 450 hp

Specifications and Performance

Cabin Biplane
Wing Span: 46' 6"
Length: 31' 9"
Range: 425 statute miles
Empty Weight: 3,155 lbs

Payload: 4 Passengers or 720 lbs
Maximum Speed: 136 mph
Cruising Speed: 115 mph

Max. A.U.W: 4,750 lbs

G-EAQS

c/n P.5E
C of A 29 March 1920

Acquired January 1920. First flight on London-Paris route 1 March 1920. C of A lapsed December 1920, scrapped 1922

G-EARU

c/n P.59
C of A 21 May 1920

Acquired 29 March 1920. Damaged in forced landing at Swanley. 10 June 1920.[28]
C of A lapsed December 1920

---

[28] see page 76

G-EASW
c/n P.6
C of A March 1919

Acquired December 1919. Engine failure in mid-Channel, 2 July 1920.[29]
Probably sold to Far East, April 1921

---

[29] see page 78

Airco 18 Limousine

Napier Lion Engine, 450 hp

Specifications and Performance

Cabin Biplane
Wing Span: 51' 3"
Length: 39' 0"
Range: 425 statute miles
Empty Weight: 4.015 lbs

Payload: 8 Passengers
Maximum Speed: 128 mph
Cruising Speed: 100 mph

Max. A.U.W: 7,000lbs

G-EARI

c/n E.52
C of A July 1922

Prototype, acquired 5 March 1920. Crashed 16 August 1920 at Wallington

G-EARO

c/n 53
C of A 15 September 1920

Acquired 21 May 1920 To the Air Council, March 1921 and later to the Instone Airline.placed in storage, September 1922. To RAE Farnborough, withdrawn from use 1928

G-EAUF

"City of Paris"

c/n E 54

C of A 11 August 1920

Acquired 31 July 1920. Crashed in France, 13 May 1921

Miscellaneous Airco Aircraft

Airco DH4R
K141 /
G-EAEW

Acquired 16 June 1919. Winner of Hendon Aerial Derby, 21 June 1919. flown by Capt. Gathergood. Broke World Closed Circuit Speed Record at 123.3 mph. C of A not issued, scrapped 1920

Airco DH 4R
K142 /
G-EAEX

Acquired 16 June 1919. Third in Hendon Aerial Derbt, 1919. C of A not issued, scrapped 1920

Airco DH 9R
K172 /
G-EAHT

Acquired 23 July 1919. Flown to the ELTA exhibition at Amsterdam in August 1919 by Capt Gathergood in the record time of 2 hr 25 min. Broke a series of British Air Speed Records at Hendon, November 1919.

BE2E
G-EAGH
Previously C 7101

Acquired July 1919. Withdrawn from use, Sept 1920.

Airco DH 6
K 100 /
G-EAAB

Owned by Airco and flown by Capt Gathergood at Hendon Race Meetings 1919

Airco DH 10
G-EAJO
Previously E 5488

Acuired 18 August 1919. Demonstrated at ELTA Exhibition, Amsterdam, by Capt Gathergood. Operated an Air Mail Service Hendon-Newcastle-Renfrew during rail strike in 1919. Written-off in forced landing in the Pyrenees, 3 March 1920.

Airco DH 10C
E 5557

Acquired June 1919. Operated Air Mail Service Hendon-Newcastle-Renfrew during rail strike.

Airco DH 14A
G-EAPY
Previously J 1940

Acquired November 1919. Built for attmpted flight Cairo-Cape Town but crashed at Messina, Sicily, 4 February 1921. Rebuilt following crash and sent to Martlesham Heath as J 1940, 26th April 1921.
Crashed and written-off, August 1921.

Airco DH 4
Previously F 2670

Acquired 20 September 1919. Little used, sold abroad April 1920

Airco DH 4
Previously F 2761

Acquired 20 September 1919. Little used, sold abroad April 1920

Appendix 4
Britain's First Airline Pilots

Brief details of the Pilots who flew for Aircraft Transport and Travel Ltd. Listed chronologically the order of their first flight on the London - Paris Air Service

The First Week of the regular service, 25th to 30th August 1919

Lieut. E.H. "Bill" Lawford, AFC.: Subject of this biography

Lieut. C. R. "Jim" McMullin: Served in the R.A.F. Communications Squadrons. Flew first scheduled service LeBourget-Hounslow also first London-Paris airmail, 10th/11th November 1919. Later flew for Savage Skywriting and joined Fairey Aviation as assistant test pilot January 1924, later chief test pilot 1931. Killed when Blackburn Bluebird III, G-EBWE, crashed on take-off in Belgium, 8th September 1931.

Major Cyril Patteson, MC, AFC: Formerly C.O. Of No.1 Communications Squadron. Surveyed London-Paris route 1918. Appointed Flying Manager of AirCo. Flew first scheduled service Hounslow-LeBourget. Had left aviation by the summer of 1925 and was unemployed. Offered post in the steel industry but by May 1927 was dissatisfied as he was unable to use his knowledge of motors and aeroplanes in this job.

Lieut. Henry "Jerry" Shaw: Born 17 November 1892. R.Ae.C. Certificate 4158. First flight 21st November 1916 in M.F.S.H., 51 Reserve Sqdn. Flew BE2's, Bristol Fighters, D.H.4, RE 8, FE 2D, Sopwith Camel, SE 5a and H.P. 0/400 in R.F.C.& R.A.F. Served in the Communications Sqdns., by January 1919 had about 400 hours experience, made last flight for R.A.F. on 1st June 1919. Joined Airco as Chief Pilot and made first flight for the company in K 109 on 8th June1919. Tested Airco 10, Airco 16 prototype and D.H.14A . Flew first charter flight Hendon-LeBourget, 15th July 1919. Left Airco November 1920, continued to fly freelance, including some test flying for deHavilland, joined Shell Mex, autumn 1921, and became their Manager at Croydon. Made last flight as pilot 23rd October 1938. Retired 1953, Died 1977.

Capt. Alan I. Riley, AFC: Born 9 December 1897. R.F.C./R.A.F. 1916 to 1919. Served in the R.A.F. Communications Sqdns. Left A.T.&T. 1920. Re-joined R.A.F. 1923/28. Joined Westland Aircraft as a Test Pilot 1928, later appointed Instructor to the Delhi Flying Club, India.

Capt. Dudley Baylis: Flew first A.T.&T. Air Mail, 11 November 1919. Left aviation on the demise of A.T.&T.and went into business.

Capt. Gerald Gathergood: Born 1895. Transferred from the Durham Light Infantry to the R.F.C., August 1915. Later delivery and test pilot at Farnborough and Martlesham Heath. Joined Airco as Test Pilot, May 1919. First place in 1919 Aerial Derby flying Airco 4R. Achieved World Closed Circuit Speed Record. Captured 18 British records for closed circuit flight, November 1919. Retired from flying December 1919 and to train as a dental surgeon. Died 21st May 1966.

These were the pilots who flew during the first week of Aircraft Transport and Travel's London - Paris Air Service from 25th to 31st August 1919. They were also the only pilots to fly on the route for Aircraft Transport and Travel Ltd until 15th September 1919

15th September 1919 to December 1920

Mr. Square: Joined A.T.&T. Sepember 1919

George B. Powell: Served in the R.A.F. Communications Squadrons. Joined A.T.&T. September 1919. Joined Instones 1921. Later Imperial Airways. Died in motoring accident, April 1925

Alan C. Campbell-Orde, AFC: Born 4th October 1898. 1916/19 R.N.A.S. & R.A.F. Served in the R.A.F Communications Sqdns. A.T.&T. September 1919 to 1920. Instructor to the Chinese Government at Peking, 1921-1923. Test Pilot Armstrong-Whitworth Ltd. 1924. Appointed Operations Manager, British Airways, December 1936, Later Director and Operations Manager, B.O.A.C. Retired 31 December 1957.

Lieut. H. W. Chattaway, AFC: R.N.A.S./R.A.F. 1917-1919. Joined A.T.&T. September 1919. Joined Instones 1921 - 1922. Appointed CATO at Croydon, after departure of Stanley Davis, June 1922 and later Deputy Chief Aerodrome Officer at Croydon in 1934. Left Croydon in 1935 and joined the Colonial Service in Singapore when he failed to be appointed as Chief Aerodrome Officer on the retirement of Major Richards.Later committed suicide.

Lieut. Frank T. Courtney: Joined September 1919. Test flew Airco 18 prototype G-EARI. Left A.T.&T. during July 1920 and formed the short lived Air Post of Banks using an AirCo 4A. Later flew for the Daimler Airway

Lieut. William Armstrong: Born 4th February 1887. Served in the R.F.C & R.A.F. Joined A.T.&T October 1919. Became a qualified pharmacist. Later Imperial Airways and B.O.A.C.

Lieut. Lindley: Joined October 1919

Lieut Lines: Joined October 1919. Left aviation to work in the cinema industry.

Lieut. Tebbit: Joined October 1919, fatally injured at Hamble in 1924 whilst attempting to reach the aerodrome with a failing engine.

Lieut. S.B. Bradley: Joined November 1919. "B" Licence No.88. Fatally injured when attempting to land Airco 4A G-EAHF at Kenley in poor weather, 11th December 1919.

Rev. P. Donald Robbins A.F.C.: Joined November 1919. Later joined Instones 1921. Also test pilot for the Aircraft Disposal Company. Left aviation to become a priest. Honorary Chaplin to G.A.P.A.N, 1929.

Lieut. Harold "Daddy" Game A.F.C.: Joined November 1919, joined Instone Airline 1920, left aviation in May 1923 and set-up a poultry breeding business.

Capt. Derek Shepperson: Served RFC/RAF. Joined April 1920. Later flew for Air Post of Banks and Instone Airline. Killed in a crash 16th September 1923 at Nashville, Tennessee, USA, flying a Savage Skywriting SE5a.

Capt. Cyril "Cy" Holmes: Born 17th April 1895. Seconded to R.F.C. 1916. Joined A.T.&T. 1920, pilot of DH 18, G-EARI, when it crashed at Wallington, 16th August 1920. Joined KLM 1921 after A.T.&T's demise, and then flew for Instone 1921 to 1923. Later test pilot for Bristol Aviation.

Robin Duke: Pilot with B.A.T. 1919. Demonstrated F.K. 26 "Big Bat" prototype at ELTA. Joined KLM and later the Daimler Airway following A.T.&T.'s demise. Killed in mid-air collision flying DH18, G-EAWO, near Grandvilliers, France, 7th April 1921

Appendix 5 Documents

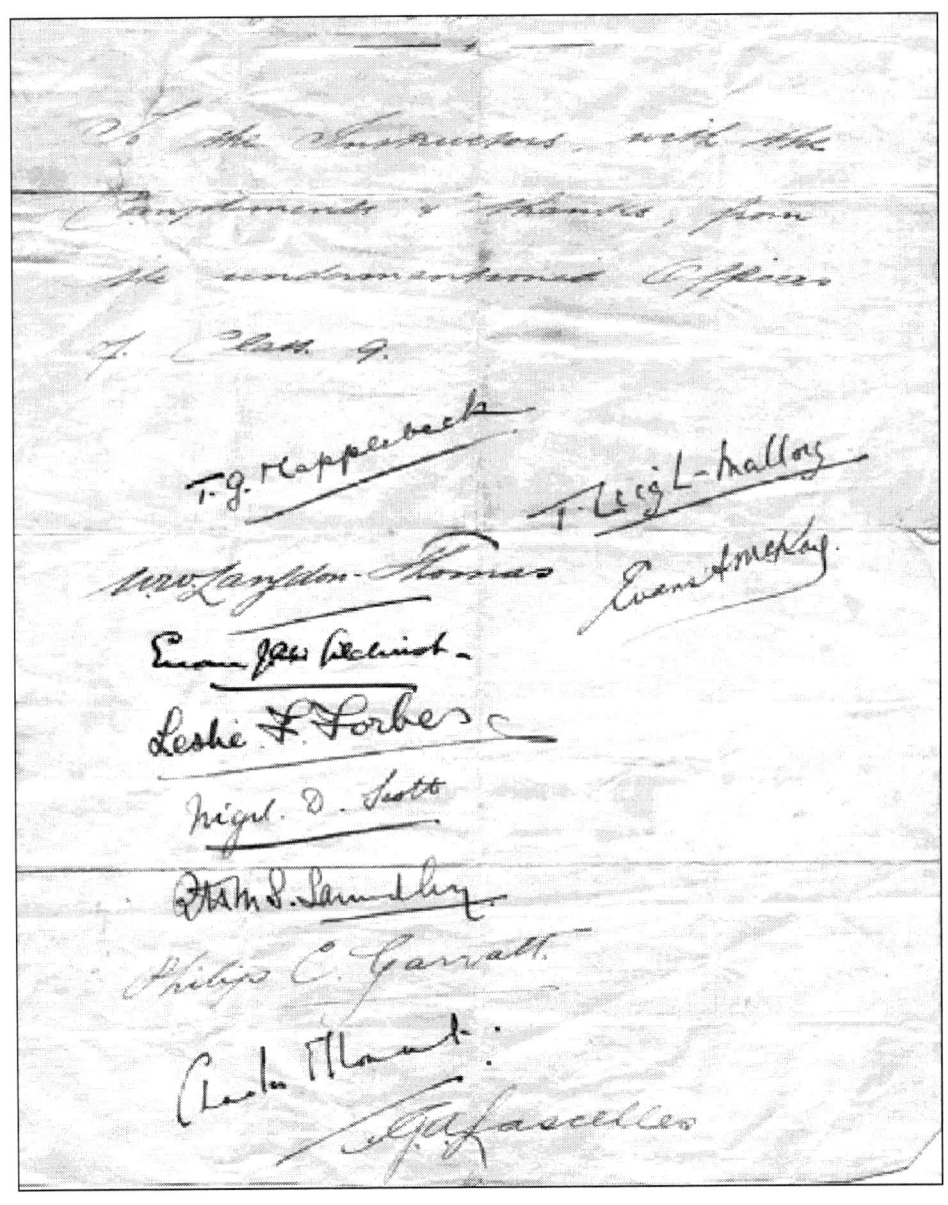

A note to the Insructors of Class 9, Reading School of Military Aeronautics. Trafford Leigh Mallory and Robert Saundby became Air Marshals holding important R.A.F. Commands during World War 2. T.G. Mapplebeck was shot down in an FE8 during November 1916 and taken prisoner. Euan Gilchrist later became an instructor at the Gosport School and C.O. of No. 60 Squadron.

E.H. Lawford Archive

Appendix 5 Documents

AIRCRAFT TRANSPORT & TRAVEL LTD.,

Telp: VICTORIA 7932

27, BUCKINGHAM GATE,
LONDON, S.W. 1.

25th September 1919.

TO ALL WHOM IT MAY CONCERN.

This is to certify that Lieut: E.H. Lawford is proceeding to Holland on behalf of this Company, for the purpose of reconnoitring the ground with a view to hiring suitable sites for aerodromes and landing grounds.

p.p. AIRCRAFT TRANSPORT & TRAVEL, LTD.

Letter of Authorisation from A.T.&T's Traffic Manager, Donald Greig, to Bill Lawford re-visit to Holland

E.H. Lawford Archive

Appendix 5 Documents

London-Paris
Air Express

Mails—Parcels—Passengers

DAILY TIME TABLE.

HOUNSLOW (depart) 12.30 p.m.	LE BOURGET (depart) 12.30 p.m.
LE BOURGET (arrive) 2.45 p.m.	HOUNSLOW (arrive) 2.45 p.m.

Mails

By arrangement with the British and French Post Offices an express airmail is now carried daily on this route. The fee is 2s. 6d. an ounce, over and above the usual rates of postage, and letters which are handed in during the morning in London, up to the times indicated, and at the Post Offices specified below, will be delivered in Paris by about 4 p.m. the same afternoon.

G.P.O., King Edward's Buildings, 11 a.m.; Threadneedle Street, 10.45 a.m.; Lombard Street, 10.45 a.m.; Parliament Street, 10.45 a.m.; Charing Cross 10.50 a.m.; W.C. District Office, 11.10 a.m.; W. District, 11.15 a.m.; S.W. District Office, 10.40 a.m.

Passengers

The passenger fares are as follows:—Single, £21; return, £42. This fare includes free conveyance by motor-car to Hounslow Aerodrome from any point within a mile of Piccadilly Circus, and also conveyance by motor from Le Bourget into Paris. Similar arrangements exist as to the journey from Paris to London. A passenger, called for at an hotel in London at 11 a.m., arrives at the door of his hotel in Paris by 4 p.m. the same afternoon.

Parcels

The rate for parcels is 5s. lb.; but in the case of parcels weighing more than 2 lbs., or for regular consignments, much lower rates can be quoted. If handed in up to 10 a.m. at the agents specified below, parcels will reach Paris the same afternoon; whereas by land and sea, even if a special "Grand Vitesse" fee is paid, a parcel is several days, and perhaps a week, in reaching its destination.

Full particulars regarding freights can be obtained from Aircraft Transport and Travel, Ltd., 25-27, Old Queen Street, S.W.1., or from the American Express Co., Queen Street and Haymarket; Thos. Cook & Son, Ludgate Circus, E.C., and 38-39, Piccadilly, W.; General Transport, Ltd., 52, Crutched Friars; J. Jackson & Sons, 7-8, Charing Cross, and King William Street, E.C.; Henry Johnson & Sons, 18, Byward Street, and Beak Street, W.; Carter Paterson & Co., 6, Maddox Street, W., and 3, Cannon Street, E.C.; Lep Aerial Travel, Piccadilly Circus (Criterion Corner); and Hernu, Peron & Co., 98-100, Queen Victoria Street, E.C.

NOTE.—Parcels are received up to 10.30 a.m. at the two depots mentioned above of the American Express Company; or up to as late as 11.30 a.m. at the Hounslow Aerodrome.

LONDON:	PARIS:
AIRCRAFT TRANSPORT & TRAVEL, LTD.,	COMPAGNIE GÉNÉRALE TRANSAERIENNE,
25-27, Old Queen Street, S.W.1.	118, Champs Elysées.

This advertisement appeared in the "Aeroplane" during December 1919 detailing A.T.&T's service and charges. The preference given to Mails and Parcels indicates their importance to the revenues of the Company

Appendix 5 Documents

AIRCRAFT TRANSPORT & TRAVEL LTD.,
"A I R C O."

Telp: VICTORIA 7932.
Purley, 1180.
FS/KS.

25, 26, 27, OLD QUEEN STREET,
LONDON, S.W.1.

23rd. September, 1920.

Mr. E. H. Lawford,
9, Mapesbury Road,
BRONDESBURY, N.W.2.

Dear Lawford,-

    Your letter of Resignation arrived to-day, and it is with very sincere regret that we shall part company.

    Your record with the A.T. & T. during its very trying times has been such that you can always be proud of it.

    Your care, endurance and knowledge of the game as a Pilot was what influenced me to put you into a position of greater responsibility, which duties you undertook with your natural energy and zeal.

    In thanking you for your efforts on my behalf please accept my very best wishes for the future.

Yours sincerely,

Frank Searle
MANAGING DIRECTOR.
AIRCRAFT TRANSPORT & TRAVEL, LIMITED.

Aircraft Transport and Travel's Managing Director. Frank Searle's reply to Bill Lawford's letter of resignation. The use of out of date headed notepaper indicated the Company's precarious financial position

E.H.Lawford Archive

Appendix 5 Documents

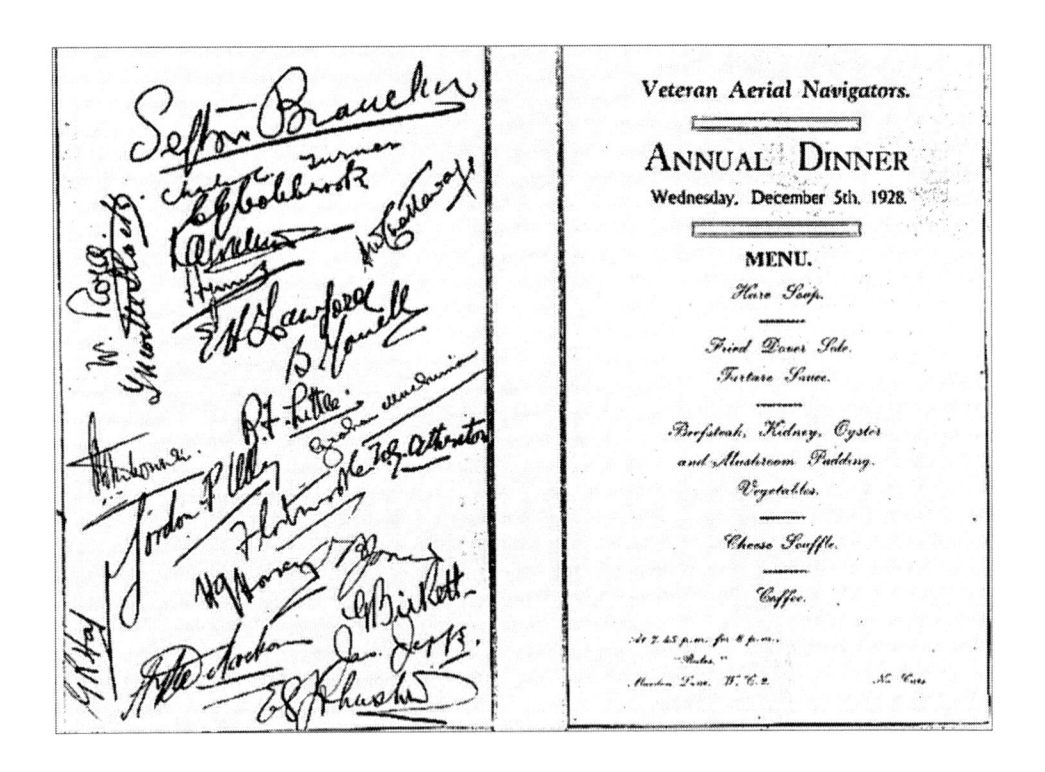

Signed Menu from the "Veteran Aerial Navigator's" Annual Dinner held at Rules Restaurant during December 1929

Among those present:

Sir W. Sefton Brancker, DCA, Charles C. Turner, C.G. Colebrooke, L.A. Walters, Walter Rogers, G.Neville Stack, E.H. "Bill" Lawford, H.W. Chattaway, Jimmy Youell, R.F. Little, Graham Mackinnon, N.G. Atherton, F. Entwhistle, Gordon P. Olley, H.G. Horsey. O.P. Jones, A.S. Wilcockson, G. Birkett Jimmy Jeffs, "Scruffy" Robinson.

Appendix 5 Documents

Charles Dickson's caricature of Bill Lawford was one of a series displayed for many years on the wall of the Pilot's Room at the Croydon Aerodrome Hotel. Bill is depicted in his well known Austin Seven sports car which was fitted with many unusual gagets.

Via Croydon Airport Society

Appendix 6

Air Ministry Officers in Charge at Croydon, 1920 to 1936

Major S.T.L. Greer: Transferred to Croydon following the closure of Hounslow. Resigned from the Air Ministry in April 1922 to become Station Manager at Brussels for the Instone Airway.

Capt. Stanley Baker: Deputy CATO at Hounslow then Croydon under Major Greer. Appointed chief CATO, Croydon, April 1922 following resignation of Major Greer. Removed from his position following a misinterpreted remark concerning Lady Maud Hoare's coat during the departure of the first service to India, December 1926. Took up a position in the transport industry.

Commander C.T. Deacon RN: At Croydon 1922. Appointed Air Ministry representative at Lympne April 1922. C.A.T.O. i/c Lympne, July 1925. Temporary Chief C.A.T.O. Croydon December 1926 to May 1927 until Major Richards appointment. Left Lympne end of 1936

Major Leslie Fitzroy Richards: Licencing Dept. At Air Ministry. Succeeded Capt. Stanley Baker as Chief CATO at Croydon, May 1927. Retired December 1935 due ill health.

Air Commodore E.H. Robinson: Appointed Chief Aerodrome Officer at Croydon following Major Richard's retirement in December 1935.

Air Ministry Civil Air Traffic Officers at Croydon 1920 to 1936

Mr. Stanley Davies: Formerly CATO at Lympne. Appointed Deputy CATO at Croydon, April 1922. Left to go to university, June 1922.

Capt. John P. Morkham: Ex-RFC/RAF. Appointed to Croydon, April 1922. Temporary secondment to Lympne, July 1925.

Capt. James P. "Jimmy" Jeffs: October 1916, observer RNAS, April 1918, RAF. Joined Air Ministry, October 1919. Appointed to Croydon as Aerodrome Traffic Control Officer, April 1922. Temporarily i/c Lympne, 1927, returned to Croydon 1928. Transferred to Heston as Chief Aerodrome Officer, November 1935. Appointed first Superintendent of Air Traffic Control, December 1937.

Granted Air Traffic Comtrollers Licence No.1. Later Commandant of Prestwick and Heathrow Airports.

Lieut. H. W. Chattaway, AFC: R.F.C./R.A.F. 1917-1919 Joined A.T.&T. September 1919, Instones 1921 - 1922. Appointed CATO at Croydon, after departure of Stanley Davis, June 1922 and later Deputy Chief Aerodrome Officer at Croydon in 1934. Left Croydon in 1935 and joined the Colonial Service in Singapore when he failed to be appointed as Chief Aerodrome Officer on the retirement of Major Richards.

E.H. "Bill" Lawford: Appointed CATO at Croydon 1924, full career details herein

Sqdn. Ldr. E.L. Johnson AFC: Appointed as a temporary Aerodrome Officer at Croydon for summer 1929, later lost in the R.101 disaster.

Arthur L. Russell: Learned to fly Ewen School, R.AeC. Aviators Cert. 406, 1913. RFC/RAF 1913 - 1927. Appointed as a temporary Aerodrome Officer at Croydon for summer 1933 and retained on a permanent basis at the end of 1934. Appointed Area Control Officer at Manchester, October 1937. Chief Control Officer, Southampton Airport, 1939

Frederick H. Robinson: Pilot RFC/RAF. Appointed Aerodrome Officer at Croydon, 1934, in charge of Flying Control School 1937.

G.W. Monk: Appointed Aerodrome Officer Grade III, 1st April 1935

R.C.I. Pearce: Appointed aerodrome officer at Croydon 1935 following the departure of H.W. Chattaway.

Radio Operators at Croydon, 1920 - 1936

W.A.G. Price: Appointed 1920. Left Croydon to take up new position at Pulham following installation of direction finding equipment in May 1922.

F.S. Mockford: Formerly a wireless officer in the RFC/RAF. Joined Air Ministry at Hounslow where he installed the first civil radio equipment. Devised the first official phonetic alphabet. Chief radio operator at Croydon from May 1922.

L. Lugar: Appointed 1920

F.S. Close: Appointed 1920

C.V. Lane: Appointed 1920

Appendix 7

Aircraft Types flown by Bill Lawford

Deperdussin Monoplane	28 hp Anzani
Caudron Biplane	35 hp Anzani & 80 hp Gnome
Henry Farman Box Kite	50 hp Gnome
Champel Biplane	100hp Anzani
Bleriot Monoplane	28 hp Anzani, 50 hp Gnome & 80hp Gnome
BE 2b	75 hp Renault
BE2c	90 hp R.A.F.
BE2d	90 hp R.A.F
BE2e	90 hp R.A.F.
Maurice Farman Longhorn	75 & 80 hp Renault
Maurice Farman Shorthorn	75 & 80 hp Renault
Avro 504	50 hp Gnome & 110 hp LeRhone & 110hp Monosoupape
RE 7	140 hp R.A.F. & 160 hp R.A.F.
RE 8	140 hp R.A.F.
Martinsyde	160 hp A.D.
FE 2b	120 & 160 hp A.D.
FE 2c	140 hp R.A.F.
FE 2d	160 A.D. & 300 hp Rolls-Royce
BE 12	140 hp R.A.F.
BE 12a	140 hp R.A.F.

Aircraft	Engine
Armstrong Whitworth FK 7	90 hp R.A.F., 140 hp R.A.F. & 160 hp A.D.
Sopwith Camel	110 hp & 130 hp Clerget
DH 6	90 hp R.A.F. & 80 hp Renault
DH 6 (Backstagger)	80 hp Renault
BE 12b	200 hp Hispano Suiza
DH 4	260 hp Fiat, 230 hp BHP, 300 & 400 hp Roll-Royce, R.A.F.
SE 5a	200 hp Hispano Suiza 180 hp Viper 230 hp Sunbeam Arab
SE 5a (short chord elevator)	200 hp Hispano Suiza
SE 5A (2 seater)	200 hp Hispano Suiza
Sopwith Dolphin	180 hp Viper & 200 hp Hispano Suiza
Sopwith Pup	110 hp LeRhone
Armstrong	130 hp Lorraine Dietrich
Handley Page 0/400	800 hp Rolls-Royce
Bristol Fighter	230 hp BHP, 250 hp Rolls-Royce, 230hp Sunbeam Arab, 180 hp Hispano Suiza
Airco DH 9	230 hp BHP, Armstrong-240hp Siddeley Puma
Sopwith Snipe	230 hp BR2
Airco DH 4a	360 hp Rolls-Royce Eagle 8
Airco DH 16	360 hp Rolls-Royce Eagle 8, 450 hp Napier Lion
Airco DH 9a	450 hp Napier

Published Sources

Above the Trenches
Christopher Shores, Norman Franks & Russell Guest   Grub Street, 1990

Airfields and Airmen, Ypres
Mike O'Connor & Leo Cooper   Pen & Sword 2001

Coming in to Land
Tim Sherwood   Heritage Publications 1999

CFS - Birthplace of Air Power
J.W.R. Taylor   Putnam 1953

Croydon Airport and the Battle for Britain 1939-1940
Douglas Cluett, Joanna Bogle & Bob Learmonth   London Borough of Sutton Libraries and Arts Services 1984

Croydon Airport Remembered
Charles C. Dickson   London Borough of Sutton Libraries and Arts Services 1985

Croydon Airport: The Great Days 1928 - 1939
Douglas Cluett, Joanna Nash & Bob Learmonth   London Borough of Sutton Libraries and Arts Services 1980

De Havilland, the Golden Years 1919 – 1939
Richard Riding   I.P.C. 1981

History of British Aviation 1908 – 1914
R. Dallas Brett   Air Research Publications 1988

History of the Guild of Air Pilots and Air Navigators 1929 – 1964. David B. Brown   G.A.P.A.N. 1967

Islands in Danger
Alan Wood & Mary Seaton Wood   Evans Brothers 1965

Milestones of Flight
M.J.H. Taylor & David Mondey   Janes Pub.Co. 1983

Recollections of an Airman
Louis Strange

John Hamilton   1933

The Airmen Who Would Not Die
John G. Fuller

Corgi Books 1981

The First Croydon Airport 1915 - 1928
Douglas Cluett, Joanna Nash & Bob Learmonth

London Borough of
Sutton Libraries
and Arts Services 1977

RFC Communiques 1915- 16
Christopher Cole

Kimber 1969

Shoreham Airport, Sussex
T.M.A. Webb & Dennis L. Bird

Cirrus Associates 1996

Sefton Branker
Norman MacMillan

Heinemann 1935

The Royal Flying Corps in France
Ralph Barker

Constable & Co. 1994

Three Score Years and Ten, 1922 - 1992
Peter Maher

Lancashire Aero Club
Barton, 1992

Wings Across the World
Harald Penrose

Cassell London 1980

World War One
Philip Warner

Cassell plc 1998

Magazines and Periodicals

Flight, Aeroplane, Aeroplane Monthly, Air Enthusiast, Pilot Magazine, Putnam Aeronautical Review, Guild News GAPAN, Croydon Airport Society Journal, Croydon Airport Society Newsletter, B.E.A Magazine, Airways, Strand Magazine, Cross and Cockade Journal, Flypast.

Other Sources

A.T.&T Traffic Book	Royal Air Force Museum, Hendon
A History of Air Traffic Control	John Platt
Logbooks, Papers and Manuscripts	Capt. E.H. "Bill" Lawford
Papers of L.A. Strange DSO OBE MC DFC	Royal Air Force Museum, Hendon
Logbooks of Capt. Henry "Jerry" Shaw	Royal Air Force Museum, Hendon
Various Documents	National Archives, Kew, Richmond, Surrey

    I would like to acknowledge the help and encouragement of Tom Samson, Peter Skinner, Mike Marshall, Geoff Hare, Larry Williamson and John King of the Croydon Airport Society, Mick Davis, Richard T. Riding and the long suffering Evelyn who has put up with me during the many hours spent at the computer while compiling this book.